Praise for Black Book of Canadian Foreign Policy

"A must-read." *Halifax Chronicle Herald*

"Leftist gadfly tears dow[n] ... *Ottawa ...*

"Encyclopedic look at C[anada] ...

"The best gift I could ha[ve] ... ['r]ears
as a foreign affairs jour[nalist] ... [...]sse."
Jooneed Khan, *Montreal ...*

"Broad in scope and packing many a punch, The Black Book of Canadian Foreign Policy is likely to become an important reference for international solidarity activists." *Montreal Hour*

"Engler presents an impressive cascade of evidence that Canada is not exactly a force for good in the world." *Montreal Review of Books*

"A book that has been desperately needed for a long time." *New Socialist*

"Persuasive, well researched, sweeping historical critique of Canadian foreign policy." *Peoples Voice*

"Whatever your politics, it's hard to put down The Black Book without seriously questioning Canada's image." *Concordia Link*

"An extremely interesting and quite largely convincing book." *rabble.ca*

"Engler's book is written in a concise, straightforward style that mostly lets the meticulously referenced facts speak for themselves." *zmag.org*

First printing Feb. 2010
Cover by Working Design
Printed and bound in Canada by Transcontinental Printing

A co-publication of
RED Publishing
2736 Cambridge Street
Vancouver, British Columbia V5K 1L7 and
Fernwood Publishing
32 Oceanvista Lane
Black Point, Nova Scotia B0J 1B0
and 8 - 222 Osborne Street, Winnipeg, Manitoba R3L 1Z3.
www.fernwoodpublishing.ca

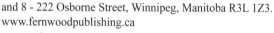

Fernwood Publishing Company Limited gratefully acknowledges the financial support of the Department of Canadian Heritage, the Nova Scotia Department of Tourism and Culture and the Canada Council for the Arts for our publishing program.

Library and Archives Canada Cataloguing in Publication
Engler, Yves, 1979-
Canada and Israel : building apartheid / Yves Engler.
Co-publisher: RED Pub.
Includes bibliographical references.
ISBN 978-1-55266-355-4
1. Canada--Foreign relations--Israel. 2. Israel--Foreign
relations--Canada.
I. Title.
FC251.I7E55 2010   **327.7105694**
C2010-900019-6

Table of Contents

Introduction

Most Canadians believe our country acts and has acted as an honest broker or peacekeeper on the world stage. While this belief may indicate a widespread desire for a democratic and humanistic foreign policy it often does not reflect reality. My *Black Book of Canadian Foreign Policy* was a broad overview of the subject. This work, on the other hand, is an attempt to understand Canada's role in one of the world's longest standing conflicts. To develop a peace-promoting, altruistic Canadian foreign policy, the first step is to understand the past and current reality. Only then can we demand change. The aim of this book is to educate Canadians about what has been and is currently being done in our name in an important part of the world.

Thousands of books describe various aspects of the Palestinian/Israeli conflict. Only a handful detail Canada's ties to the dispute and most do so from a pro-Israel perspective. This is the first book to focus on Canadian support for the dispossession of Palestinians, for a state building a nation based on one religion, and for the last major European colonial project.

Most Canadians believe their government should treat all citizens equally and that everyone born in Canada is Canadian. They support the Charter of Rights and Freedoms, which bans discrimination based on religion, ethnicity and place of origin. A majority believes multiculturalism is a good a thing and are proud that people from all religious backgrounds, from every ethnicity and from every corner of the globe can be accepted as Canadian. Our constitution recognizes, and most of us believe, that First Nations have rights to their land and self-government. Despite numerous ongoing abuses, many Canadians regret the historical treatment of indigenous people and our colonial past. The federal government has apologized for some of its most egregious past behaviour.

I believe most Canadians want their government to uphold the Charter of Rights and Freedoms by following its principles when determining our foreign policy. Yet, in many respects Israel represents the antithesis of these principles. It proclaims itself a nation of one religion. It controls millions of people's lives without allowing them to vote. It refuses to allow hundreds of thousands of people born in the land of Israel and their descendents to become citizens or even visit the country. In many ways Israel's current reality resembles the worst of Canada's colonial past.

Still, this book is not about Israel, or the nature of Zionism. It does, however, begin with the position that Israel is an "apartheid state".[1] In recognition that this analysis is controversial in some quarters, a short explanation is necessary.

In *Palestine: Peace Not Apartheid* former U.S. President Jimmy Carter argues that Israel's policies in the Palestinian territories constitute "a system of apartheid, with two peoples occupying the same land, but completely separated from each other, with Israelis totally dominant and suppressing violence by depriving Palestinians of their basic human rights."[2] On numerous occasions Nobel Peace Prize winner Archbishop Desmond Tutu has compared the treatment of Palestinians to Blacks under South African apartheid. The 1973 UN International Convention on the Suppression and Punishment of the Crime of Apartheid described the "inhuman acts" of apartheid as:

"Denial to a member or members of a racial group or groups of the right to life and liberty of persons... By the infliction upon the members of a racial group or groups of serious bodily or mental harm, by the infringement of their freedom or dignity, or by subjecting them to torture or to cruel, inhuman or degrading treatment or punishment.

"Any legislative measures and other measures calculated to prevent a racial group or groups from participation in the political, social, economic and cultural life of the country ... including ... the right to education, the right to leave and to return to their country, the right to a nationality, the right to freedom of movement and residence.

"Any measures, including legislative measures, designed to divide the population along racial lines by the creation of separate reserves and ghettos for the members of a racial group or groups ... the expropriation of landed property belonging to a racial group."[3]

Certain aspects of Israeli reality fit this definition. Israel's laws are fundamentally racist, forcing citizens and institutions to make racist decisions. "Legal apartheid is regulated in Israel," notes Uri Davis, by "ceding state sovereignty and investing its responsibilities in the critical area of immigration, settlement and land development with Zionist organizations constitutionally committed to the exclusive principle of 'only for the Jews'."[4] With quasi state status the World Zionist Organization, Jewish Agency and Jewish National Fund are constitutionally committed to serving and promoting the interests of Jews and only Jews.[5]

Through the Law of Return, my longtime friend in Vancouver, Michael Rosen, — who hasn't been to Israel, has no familial connection to the country and has never even been religious — can emigrate to Israel. On the other hand, Noor Tibi, a woman I met at Concordia University in Montreal whose grandfather fled from Haifa in 1948, could not enter (let alone live in) Israel until she got a Canadian passport. Justified as an affirmative action measure to protect besieged Jewry, the Law of Return becomes patently racist when Israel refuses to allow Palestinian refugees to return to their homeland.

Zionist forces expelled 87% of the Arab population from the soon-to-be Jewish state in 1947/48.[6] This was the first major act of apartheid waged against Palestinians. Refusing to allow them to return is an ongoing form of apartheid. Since its establishment Israel has been in a state of emergency to keep the properties of Palestinian refugees in the hands of the state and the Jewish

National Fund.[7] This theft is sanctified by the Absentees' Property Law of 1950.[8]

Most of the land Israel grabbed from Palestinians is off limits to the Arabs who remain in Israel. Almost a fifth of the population, Arabs are legally excluded from owning 93% of Israel (not including the occupied territories).[9] They are also politically disenfranchised. Between 1948 and 1966 the Arab sectors of Israel were under martial law and today political parties that oppose the Jewish supremacist character of the state are outlawed.[10] Article 7 (a) of Israel's Basic Law stipulates that "A candidates' list shall not participate in the elections to the Knesset if its objects or actions, expressly or by implication, include... negation of the existence of the State of Israel as the state of the Jewish people."[11]

In addition to legal structures that discriminate against the indigenous Arab population, government services prioritize Jews. Despite making up 18% of the population, Arab Israelis receive about 4% of public spending.[12] A March 2009 report found that the "government invested [US] $1,100 in each Jewish pupil's education compared to $190 for each Arab pupil. The gap is even wider when compared to the popular state-run religious schools, where Jewish pupils receive nine times more funding than Arab pupils."[13] According to Israel's National Insurance Institute, half of all Arab Israeli families live in poverty compared to 14% of Jewish families.[14]

In the West Bank, Israeli apartheid is especially obvious. The population has been pushed into bantustan-like enclaves, encircled by a massive wall, had their water and land appropriated, and are subjected to daily humiliation at military checkpoints. For more than four decades supposedly democratic Israel has dominated the West Bank population without allowing them to vote in national elections. In Gaza 1.5 million Palestinians — many of whom were forced from their homes in 1947/48 — live in a giant prison cut off from the world by the mighty Israeli military.

In fact, Zionism is an expansionist settler ideology. For more than a century the Zionist movement has steadily usurped Arab land. Many Zionists believe Eretz Israel (the land of Israel) includes the West Bank, Gaza and much more. The 450,000 state-supported settlers illegally installed in the West Bank and East Jerusalem are an expression of this expansionism.[15] So is Israel's annexation of the Golan Heights, which was captured from Syria in the 1967 war.

To achieve its aims this expansionist ideology requires military might ("Israel is an army with a state" goes the saying). Israel has bombed Syria, Palestine, Jordan, Egypt, Sudan, Lebanon, Tunisia, Iraq and threatens to bomb Iran. Israeli military historian Zeev Maoz explains: "Between 1948 and 2004, Israel fought six interstate wars, fought two (some say three) civil wars, and engaged in over 144 dyadic militarized interstate disputes (MIDs) that involved the threat, the display, or the use of military force against another state. Israel is by far the most conflict prone state in modern history. It has averaged nearly four MIDS every year. It has fought an interstate war every nine years. Israel appears on top of the list of the most intense international rivalries in the last 200-year period."[16] Later in *Defending The Holy Land: A Critical Analysis of Israel's Security & Foreign Policy*, Maoz notes: "There was only one year out of 56 years of history in which Israel did not engage in acts involving the threat, display, or limited use of force with its neighbors. The only year in which Israel did not engage in a militarized conflict was 1988, when Israel was deeply immersed in fighting the Palestinian uprising, the intifada. So it is fair to say that during each and every year of its history Israel was engaged in violent military actions of some magnitude."[17] Maoz concludes: "None of the wars — with a possible exception of the 1948 war of Independence — was what Israel refers to as Milhemet Ein Brerah ('war of necessity'). They were all wars of choice or wars of folly."[18]

This book will demonstrate that, with the exception of Israel's 1956 invasion of Egypt, Ottawa openly or tacitly endorsed these military endeavors. Despite claims to the contrary, Canada is not, nor has it ever been, an "honest broker" in the Palestine-Israel conflict. The different elements that make up Canada's foreign policy – from diplomacy to security services, to tax policies related to charities, to "non-governmental organizations" such as churches – have largely sided with Israel.

This book will argue that, from the beginning, Israel was primarily the creation of European/North American sociopolitical forces, including Canadian ones. Ideologically, Zionism's roots come from biblical literalism and European nationalism. Both also played significant roles in Canadian history. Zionism can be described as the ideology of the last major European settler movement. Of course Canada is, or at least was, also a settler state, which made Israel a familiar face and garnered it support.

This book will also describe the important role Canadian diplomats played in the 1947 UN negotiations to create a Jewish state on Palestinian land. Uninterested in the welfare of the indigenous population, Lester Pearson played a central role in two different UN bodies discussing the issue and Canada's representative to the UN Special Committee on Palestine, Ivan C. Rand, pushed a partition plan bitterly resisted by Palestinians. After the UN-backed partition vote Canadians supported efforts to expel Palestine's Arab population. Hundreds of Canadians fought in the 1947/48 war, while many more financed and procured weapons. During the war 700,000 Palestinians were driven from their homeland and Israel conquered 24% more territory than it was allocated in the already generous partition plan.

This book will argue that, unmoved by Palestinian suffering, Canadian diplomacy continued its one-sided backing of Israel after the 1948 war. Ottawa actively supported Israel before, during and after the 1967 war, for instance. A number of studies in the 1980s found Canada to be among Israel's best friends at the UN. While, on occasion, Canadian pronouncements and UN votes have supported Palestinian rights, rarely have the different arms of Canadian foreign policy provided concrete support. Canadian intelligence and military services have been one-sided advocates of Israel. The Canadian Security Intelligence Service (CSIS) works closely with Mossad (its Israeli equivalent) and many Canadian weapons-makers ship their products to Israel. As well, private charities support Israeli militarism and every year Canadians send hundreds of millions of dollars worth of tax-deductible donations to Israeli universities, parks, immigration initiatives etc. More controversially, millions of dollars in private money, often subsidized by Canadian tax write-offs, is funnelled to illegal Israeli settlements in the West Bank.

This book will discuss how Canada's political culture has spurred a political party two-step in which the Conservatives and Liberals one-up each other in proclaiming their love of Israel. Both Liberal and Conservative governments — from John Diefenbaker to Lester Pearson, Brian Mulroney to Paul Martin and Stephen Harper — staunchly backed Israel. And rarely has the opposition challenged the ruling parties' positions. Even the Left has supported Zionism since World War II, which explains (part of) Canada's staunch support for Israel. The book will argue that this lack of opposition has allowed the current government to make Canada (at least diplomatically) the most pro-Israel country in the world.

Finally, this book will discuss why Canadian politicians have exhibited such one-sided support for Israel. The central reason is this country's ties to U.S.-led imperialism. Support for Israel has largely mirrored different governments' relationship to Washington.

The book concludes with a discussion of how to reverse course. We need to create a political climate where supporting the killing of Palestinians and stealing their land is no longer acceptable.

Chapter 1
The creation of Zionism

Zionism's roots are Christian, not Jewish. "Christian proto-Zionists [existed] in England 300 years before modern Jewish Zionism emerged," notes one book.[1] The Protestant Reformation's biblical literalism is what spurred Zionism. In 1649 two English Puritans in Amsterdam asked London "that this nation of England, with the inhabitants of the Netherlands, shall be the first and the readiest to transport Israel's sons and daughters on their ships to the land promised to their forefathers, Abraham, Isaac and Jacob for an everlasting inheritance."[2] This declaration is thought to be the "first time in the history of the idea of Jewish restoration that human action was put forward as the only way to achieve a goal which had previously been regarded, by Jews and non-Jews alike, as a spiritual event to be brought about only by divine intervention."[3] Until the mid-1800s Zionism was an almost entirely non-Jewish movement.[4] And yet it was quite active. Between 1796 and 1800 there were at least 50 books published in Europe about the Jews' return to Palestine.[5]

Zionism's roots in Canada are Christian as well. At the time of Confederation Canada's preeminent Christian Zionist was Henry Wentworth Monk. Monk "took part in the first attempt at a Zionist agricultural settlement in Palestine," boasts his biography.[6] To buy Palestine from the Ottomans (Turkey) in 1875 he began the Palestine Restoration Fund.[7] Unsuccessful, seven years later Monk took out an ad in the *Jewish World* proposing a "Bank of Israel" to finance Jewish resettlement.[8] A history of the Canadian Jewish community explains: "Henry Wentworth Monk, an eccentric but respected businessman, spent much of his time and money crusading for a Jewish homeland. In the 1870s and 1880s — long before Theodore Herzl, the Austrian founder of Zionism, even thought of a Jewish state — Monk took up a campaign in Canada and England to raise funds to buy land in Palestine for European Jews. In 1881 Monk even proposed setting up a Jewish National Fund. He issued manifestoes, wrote long articles, spoke to assorted meetings and lobbied extensively in England and Canada to realize his dream."[9]

A speech in England by Anthony Ashley Cooper, Earl of Shaftesbury, in 1839 or 1840 was Monk's first encounter with Zionist thinking.[10] Shaftesbury, who came up with the infamous Zionist slogan "a land without people for a people without a land", wanted Jews to go to their "rightful home" (Palestine) under a British protectorate.[11] "The Earl of Shaftesbury was the first millennariast, or restorationist, to blend the biblical interest in Jews and their ancient homeland with the cold realities of [British imperial] foreign policy."[12] He got Britain's foreign secretary to appoint the first British consul to Jerusalem in 1839.[13]

For his part, Monk called for the British Empire to establish a "Dominion of Israel", similar to the Dominion of Canada.[14] "Monk believed that Palestine was the logical center of the British Empire, and could help form a confederation of the English-speaking world."[15] As part of his campaign to have Britain take up the Zionist cause, Monk sent a letter to A.J. Balfour (who became British Foreign Secretary and authored the Balfour Declaration) entitled "Stand Up O Jerusalem." Monk's biography notes: "At the end of his life he wrote to Lord Balfour, in 1896, a remarkable letter which contributed to the thinking that led up to the issue of the Balfour Declaration of Palestine twenty years later."[16] While there is little evidence that Balfour was indeed influenced by Monk, some of his works were read into the Canadian Senate's records.[17]

Monk was not alone in Canada. "There were a number of others, mostly clergyman but also some politicians and journalists, who took up the Zionist cause in those years."[18] Leading British Christian Zionist John Nelson Darby made seven missions to

Canada and the U.S. between 1862 and 1877 while "for many years, [Charles] Russell's popular sermons linking biblical prophecy with contemporary events [in Palestine] were reproduced in over 1500 newspapers in the USA and Canada."[19] After serving as pastor of the American church in Jerusalem, Reverend Albert Thompson, a Canadian, returned in the 1910s to lecture widely on "the Jewish colonies" in the holy land "turning the wilderness into a very garden of the Lord."[20] This was supposed to prepare the way for restoration and the second coming of Jesus.

Widely viewed as the father of Jewish Zionism, Austrian-born Theodore Herzl worked closely with leading German Christian Zionist Rev. William H. Hechler, chaplain to the British Embassy in Vienna. He arranged for Herzl to meet Germany's Kaiser Wilhelm II and the Ottoman sultan.[21] Spurred by Christian Zionism, flourishing European nationalist ideologies and growing Western involvement in the Middle East, in 1897 Herzl organized the first Zionist conference in Basel, Austria.

The next year Zionist organizations were established in Toronto, Kingston, Winnipeg, Hamilton, Ottawa, Quebec and Montreal.[22] "When the Zionist Federation was formed in Canada there was scarcely a convention that was not attended by a number of leading Canadian Christians, and there were always effusive greetings from Cabinet ministers, mayors, lieutenant governors and other officials."[23]

In 1910 the president of the Federation of Zionist Societies of Canada, Clarence De Sola, described the fortuitous political climate within which he operated. "The secular press of Canada has always been friendly to the Zionist movement. The Christians in this country, as a rule, are very friendly to Zionism as they see in it the fulfilling of prophecies which they believe in just as we do. Consequently, their newspapers give us very cordial support."[24]

Citing a mix of Christian and pro-British rationale, leading Canadian politicians repeatedly expressed support for Zionism. In

1907, two Ministers attended the Federation of Zionist Societies of Canada convention, telling delegates that "Zionism had the support of the government."[25] Solicitor General (and later Prime Minister) Arthur Meighen proclaimed in November 1915: "I think I can speak for those of the Christian faith when I express the wish that God speed the day when the land of your forefathers shall be yours again. This task I hope will be performed by that champion of liberty the world over — the British Empire."[26]

During a July 1922 speech to the Zionist Federation of Canada Prime Minister Mackenzie King "was effusive with praise for Zionism".[27] He told participants their aspirations were "in consonance" with the greatest ideals of "Englishman".[28] A dozen years later Prime Minister R.B. Bennett told a coast-to-coast radio broadcast for the launch of the United Palestine Appeal that the Balfour declaration and the British conquest of Palestine represented the beginning of the fulfillment of biblical prophecies.[29] "When the promises of God, speaking through his prophets, are that the home will be restored in the homeland of their forefathers ... Scriptural prophecy is being fulfilled. The restoration of Zion has begun."[30]

Canadian support for Zionism was largely spurred by this country's ties to Great Britain, which was Zionism's main patron for decades. Zionism grew alongside Britain's moves to assert control over the Middle East. After Britain took control of Egypt in 1882 imperial officials increasingly saw the nascent Jewish nationalist movement as a vehicle to strengthen their geostrategic position in the region. "During the last decade of the 19th century, the demands of [the British] empire also demanded political Zionism."[31] This thinking was not alien to Canada. A July 1878 *Manitoba Free Press* editorial "suggested that [British] Prime Minister [Benjamin] Disraeli might use his influence to affect the establishment of a Jewish state" to improve Britain's strategic position in the Middle East.[32]

During the last decades of Ottoman rule over Palestine British support for Zionism was relatively modest. On numerous occasions British (and other European) officials intervened with the Ottomans on behalf of Zionist settlers.[33] But, for the most part, London was unwilling to directly challenge the Ottomans. As long as Germany, France or Russia did not gain at their expense the British preferred to prop up the crumbling Ottoman Empire.[34]

Things changed during World War I. Great Britain found itself at war with the Ottomans and in January 1916, Britain and France signed a secret accord to divvy up the Ottoman-controlled Middle East.[35] Later that year British General Edmund Allenby led a campaign to take Palestine from the Ottomans. As many as 400 Canadians (about half recruited specifically for the task) fought in Allenby's Jewish Legion that helped conquer modern day Israel/Palestine.[36]

Federation of Zionist Societies of Canada President Clarence de Sola mobilized Canadian Jews to join Allenby's Jewish Legion. He "supported the project [of recruiting Canadian Jews to fight] wholeheartedly."[37] Sometimes beleagured Jewish communities were often praised by the media for taking up England's cause.[38]

Just before capturing Jerusalem, in November 1917, London released the Balfour declaration, which was the British Empire's statement of support for a Jewish homeland on land occupied mostly by Muslim and Christian Palestinians. Balfour later explained his thinking: "In Palestine we do not propose to go through the form of consulting the wishes of the present inhabitants of the country. … The four great powers are committed to Zionism and Zionism, be it right or wrong, good or bad, is rooted in age-long tradition, in present needs, in future hopes, of far profounder import than the desire and prejudices of the 700,000 Arabs who now inhabit that ancient land. In my opinion that is right."[39]

For the next two decades the British Empire provided the Zionist movement with the necessary protective umbrella to thrive.[40] As a British dominion, without an officially independent foreign policy until 1931, Canada also adhered to the Balfour declaration. (It was another, much less heralded, Balfour declaration that set Canada towards an officially independent foreign policy in 1926.) In later years some at External Affairs claimed Canada's responsibilities in relation to Palestine were unclear, but a department legal adviser noted, "this [Balfour] declaration is signed on behalf of Canada."[41] In fact, Canadian Prime Minister Robert Borden participated in a 1918 British Imperial War Cabinet meeting where the fate of Palestine was part of the agenda.[42]

Many Canadian political leaders were overjoyed by British support for Zionism. Several years after World War I Conservative party leader Arthur Meighen claimed "of all the results of the [world war] none was more important and more fertile in human history than the reconquest of Palestine and the rededication of that country to the Jewish people."[43] The fact that Canada was a proud dominion of the British Empire created an environment for Jewish Zionism to flourish. Prominent early Canadian "Jewish leaders like Clarence de Sola and Rabbi Ashinsky," notes *Taking Root*, "saw the [Zionist] movement as potentially an integral part of British imperialism."[44] De Sola informed Canada's Minister of Militia and Defence, Sidney Mewburn, that "the Jews would like to see Palestine under the suzerainty of the British government, forming thus an outlying and buffer state of the British Empire."[45]

A prominent Canadian Zionist, Rabbi Dr. Herman Abramowitz, noted in 1918: "Another star, the star of Jacob, will now shine brilliantly from the British constellation. It will be good for Great Britain because it would put in Palestine a friendly people, who would act as a buffer state, protecting the Suez Canal, India, Egypt, and trade to those countries. The cultural value of having an oriental people who, through their dispersion, had also become a western people, to mediate and create an understanding between the East and West, is the highest value of all."[46]

A number of books about Canada's Jewish community discuss how elite Canadian Jews, especially after the 1917 Balfour declaration, were more active Zionists than their U.S. counterparts. "The First World War accentuated differences between Canadian and American Jewry. For example, loyalty to Britain's cause provided Zionists with opportunities to identify their purposes with Britain's imperial mission."[47] And Canada's "established Jewish community ... were Anglophile to the core."[48] During World War I the Jewish elite enthusiastically supported Britain even though London was allied with Russia's notoriously anti-Semitic czar.[49] (At that time Zionism was largely promoted as a way for Jews to escape czarist anti-Semitism.)

In Canada, much more than in the U.S., it was beneficial to one's standing among the elite to support Zionism. In the U.S. "Zionism often appealed more to newcomers and to those whose stake in society was limited. In Europe, too, assimilating Jews usually shunned the Zionist movement in these years. In Canada, however, many prosperous, acculturated Jews were affiliated with the Zionist movement, even taking on leadership positions."[50] There was no hint of dual loyalty for Canadians who worked to create a Jewish state. Zionism could be part of "British Canadian nationalism."[51]

Jewish Zionism should be understood from within the political climate in which it operated. And Canada's political culture clearly fostered Zionist ideals. British imperialism, Christian Zionism and nationalist ideology were all part of this country's political fabric. Additionally, in the early 1900s most Canadians did not find it odd that Europeans would take a "backward" people's land. That is what settlers did to the indigenous population in Canada.

As bearers of "progress" Zionist pioneers in Palestine were viewed in a similar way to earlier British settlers in North America.[52] Leading Canadian Zionist Dr. Herman Abramowitz summarized this thinking: "Without us Palestine has given nothing to the world.

After our departure it formed an alluviun to the rest of the desert. For thirteen centuries it has housed the Arabs and they have given to the world nothing. For as many years it has received a handful of Jews, and in these years we have substituted for Machiavellianism a modern economic and living civilization; in thirteen years we have substituted for the malarial swamps and disease infested districts of thirteen centuries — modern sanitation; in thirteen years we have substituted for the illiteracy of 13 centuries a modern school system headed by a University; in thirteen years we have substituted for a land of analphabetism the publication of thousands of books; last year alone Palestine produced, as against not a single volume in thirteen centuries, three hundred and sixty five printed books — one for every day of the year."[53]

While Abramowitz's logic — we publish more books so we can steal your land — seems outrageous today, this sort of colonialist view was once widely held. In a 1945 letter quoted in the House of Commons, executive director of the Canadian Palestine Committee, Herbert Mowat, called Arabs "a primitive people."[54] Demonstrating a total disregard for the indigenous inhabitants Mowat, a Christian, continued: "There is no doubt that a policy on Palestine agreed upon by the United States, Great Britain and the other United Nations will be one to which the Arabs will be forced to adjust themselves."[55]

Once British strategic thinkers began to see Palestine as potentially valuable, Zionists became dynamic Europeans who could bring energy, skills and capital to a "derelict" region.[56] Just as French and English settlers in Canada were seen as a manifestation of god-approved European power and expansionism so too (albeit to a lesser extent) were Jewish settlers in Palestine.

Some Canadians participated in early Jewish colonialism in historic Palestine. Backed by the wealthy Rothschild family, in 1894 members of Montreal's Shavei Zion tried to start an agricultural colony in modern day Jordan.[57] Two Canadian women who emigrated in the 1930s wrote memoirs about their transition to life in Palestine.[58] Dov Joseph was the highest profile early Canadian settler in Palestine. Born in Montreal in 1899 he served in the Jewish Legion during World War I and then returned to complete a law degree at McGill. In 1921 he moved permanently to Palestine where he was the treasurer of the executive committee of the Jewish Agency and military governor of Jerusalem during the 1948 war. Joseph subsequently became a cabinet minister in several Israeli governments.[59]

But, Canada was a rich and relatively tolerant country so only a small fraction of the Jewish community emigrated to Israel. Canadians, however, underwrote a significant amount of Jewish immigration to Palestine. At first, raising money for the Zionist cause was difficult. Henry Wentworth Monk's 1875 scheme to buy Palestine from the Ottomans was unsuccessful and in 1906 Canadian Zionists raised only $6,000.[60] In 1910 the Federation of Zionist Societies launched a more ambitious scheme to buy a few thousand dunums (one dunum equalled about 920 square metres at this time) of land in the Galilee.[61] As British interest in Palestine grew fundraising became easier. Established just after Allenby's late 1917 conquest of Jerusalem, the Helping Hand Fund raised almost $160,000 in a year and the Palestine Restoration Fund also raised thousands more from Canadians.[62] Spurred by the November 1917 Balfour declaration Canadians raised $458,000 from 1919 to 1921.[63] By the mid-1940s Canadians had invested $5 million in Palestine.[64]

In the 1920s Asher Pierce of Montreal established the Gan Chayim Corporation "to develop orange plantations on the Sharon plain [between the Mediterranean Sea and the Samarian Hills], and also built a house on his own estate, which he called tel Asher."[65] At the end of that decade, Canadians put up $1 million for the lands of Wadi al-Hawarith (or Hefer Plain).[66] A 30,000 dunam stretch of coastal territory located about half way between Haifa and Tel Aviv, the land was home to a Bedouin (mostly nomadic) community of

1,000 to 1,200.[67] Without consulting the Palestinians living on the land, in 1928 the Jewish National Fund (JNF) acquired legal title to Wadi al-Hawarith from an absentee landlord in France.[68]

For four years the tenants of Wadi al-Hawarith resisted British attempts to evict them. Historian Walid Khalidi explains: "The insistence of the people of Wadi al-Hawarith to remain on their land came from their conviction that the land belonged to them by virtue of their having lived on it for 350 years. For them, ownership of the land was an abstraction that at most signified the landlords' right to a share of the crop."[69]

The conflict at Wadi al-Hawarith became a lightning rod for the growing Palestinian nationalist movement. In 1933 a general strike was organized in Nablus to support the tenants of Wadi al-Hawarith.[70] Palestinians, especially those without title to their lands, resented the European influx into their homeland.

At the turn of the century Jews made up about four percent of Palestine's population.[71] That increased to 10% in 1917, grew for a decade then stagnated between 17% and 18% from 1928 to 1932.[72] At that proportion of the population, the Zionist project was not feasible. But Hitler's 1933 rise to power caused the Jewish population to reach 30% by 1938.[73] Most German Jews would have preferred to emigrate to North America but countries such as Canada refused to accept them. By refusing to open its gate to Jews fleeing Nazi Germany Canada helped spur on the Zionist project.

In fact, a number of anti-Semitic Canadian politicians backed Zionism as a way to divert Jews from Canada. Known to support Zionism as a way to deal with the "Jewish problem," in 1934 Prime Minister R.B. Bennett opened the annual United Palestine Appeal with a coast-to-coast radio broadcast.[74] "Alberta Premier, E.C. Manning," for his part, "allowed his name to be associated with the Canadian Palestine Committee, but was known for anti-Jewish statements on his 'back to the bible' Sunday radio broadcasts."[75]

Chapter 2
The birth of the State of Israel

Under growing Zionist military pressure after World War II Britain prepared to hand its mandate over Palestine to the UN. In response, the international body formed the First Committee on Palestine, which was charged with developing the terms of reference for a committee that would find a solution for the British mandate. Canadian Undersecretary of State for External Affairs Lester Pearson, a staunch Zionist, chaired the committee that established the United Nations Special Committee on Palestine (UNSCOP) in May 1947.

Having recently concluded a term as ambassador in Washington, Pearson defined UNSCOP largely to facilitate Zionist aspirations. He rejected Arab calls for an immediate end to the British mandate and the establishment of an independent democratic country.[1] The Arab Higher Committee wanted the European Jewish refugee issue excluded from UNSCOP but Pearson worked to give the body a mandate "to investigate all questions and issues relevant to the problem of Palestine."[2] A U.S. State Department memo noted that Pearson "proved to be an outstanding chairman for [the First] Committee."[3] Opposed to the idea that representatives from Canada, Guatemala, Yugoslavia etc. should decide their future, Palestinians boycotted UNSCOP.[4]

Officially, eleven "neutral" states sent representatives to UNSCOP. In reality "most [UNSCOP] members were chosen in order to serve the interests of one or other of the superpowers."[5] Under U.S. pressure, Canada agreed to participate in UNSCOP. The State Department had two different lists of countries it wanted to participate — Canada was at the top of both of these non-alphabetical lists.[6] Britain's ambivalence towards UNSCOP made some External Affairs officials reluctant to participate but Washington maneuvered Ottawa into "a position where refusal to serve on the commission [UNSCOP] would have been awkward and embarrassing."[7]

Canada's representative to UNSCOP was Supreme Court Justice Ivan C. Rand — famous for his role in establishing the legal basis for union dues collection (the "Rand Formula"). Rand and his assistant from External Affairs, Leon Mayrand, were sympathetic to Zionism. Rand, according to Israeli historian Illan Pappé, "claimed that weighty moral issues were involved in the question of Palestine, though he was more inclined to see it as a struggle between the forces of progress and democracy on the one hand [the Jews] and backward societies on the other [the Palestinians]."[8]

Rand was an admirer of prominent American Zionist and Supreme Court judge, Louis Brandeis and a number of Canadian Jews living in Palestine apparently influenced Rand during his time on UNSCOP.[9] So did a Canadian minister, a family friend, who lived in Jerusalem. Rand wrote a forward to the Rev. William L. Hull's book. *The Fall and Rise of Israel*, which came out in 1954, explains: "We believe that true Zionism is a move of God and that those who are true Zionists with a love of the land God has given them will feel the urge to aid actively in Israel the rebuilding of Zion."[10] Later he writes: "The [Palestinian] refugees [expelled by Israel] are in Arab lands, and the Word of God says that they shall not return to their cities."[11]

Some consider Rand the principle architect of the partition plan.[12] He opposed proposals for a Jewish-Arab unitary state and made key interventions in the decision-making process in support of partition.[13] During UNSCOP's hearings Rand berated Professor Judah Magnes, a Jewish supporter of a bi-national state. "What you say is that that yearning [Zionist desire for a Jewish state] must remain forever unsatisfied."[14]

"Rand worked hard," notes his biographer, "to ensure the maximum geographical area possible for the new Jewish state."[15] At one point, Rand and another UNSCOP member, supported giving the Zionists a larger piece of land than they officially asked for.[16] Confronted about this proposal, Rand "claimed that since Britain had not fulfilled its obligations to the Jews, they deserved to be compensated by the United Nations."[17] He challenged members of UNSCOP who failed to recognize the legitimacy of the Balfour declaration. While concerned with upholding the Balfour declaration, Rand wasn't worried about abrogating Britain's World War I promise to grant the Arabs independence. Intent on upholding the Empire's earlier statements Rand was hostile to Britain's position on Zionism in 1947. Ignoring decades of British support for Zionism, he charged that London "turned her back to all her promises" to the Jews.[18] Ultimately, Rand drafted a large part of the majority report calling for partition into a Jewish and Arab state. "Justice Rand was by far the main contributor to the partition scheme with economic union," Rand's assistant, Leon Mayrand, cabled External Affairs with satisfaction.[19]

To commemorate Rand's role in furthering Zionist aspirations, in 1954 an Israeli forest was planted in his honor.[20] For his part, Rand continued to support Israel until he died in 1969. He sent regular donations to Hebrew University, which established an Ivan C. Rand Chair of Law.[21]

The majority and minority reports put forward by UNSCOP were supposed to provide the basis for the General Assembly decision on the British mandate. But the Arab countries refused to accept the way the debate and negotiations were framed. "The Arab delegations requested that before a decision be taken, the International Court of Justice be asked for its opinion on the following subjects: (a) whether or not Palestine was included in the Arab territories that had been promised independence by Britain at the end of World War I; (b) whether partition was consistent with the objectives and provisions of the [British] mandate; (c) whether partition was consistent with the principles of the UN Charter; (d) whether its adoption and forcible execution were within the competence or jurisdiction of the UN; and (e) whether it lay within the power of any UN member or group of members to implement partition without the consent of the majority of the people living within the country."[22]

Ottawa was opposed to allowing the International Court of Justice to consider these questions.[23] Canada's position was important. The UN Ad Hoc Committee voted 21 to 20 against taking the issue to the International Court.[24]

After the Arabs failed to have the issue brought before the International Court UNSCOP's majority and minority reports were sent to the special UN Ad Hoc Committee on the Palestinian Question. At the Ad-Hoc Committee's Special Committee 1 Pearson worked feverishly to broker a partition agreement acceptable to Moscow and Washington. Preoccupied with the great powers, the indigenous inhabitants' concerns did not trouble the future prime minister. Pearson dismissed solutions that didn't involve partition, which effectively meant a Jewish state on Palestinian land. Responding to a bi-national plan proposed by the Ad-Hoc Committee's Special Committee 2, he claimed, "The unitary state proposal meant nothing — a recommendation 'out of the blue and into the blue.'"[25] Pearson later explained: "I have never wavered in my view that a solution to the problem was impossible without the recognition of a Jewish state in Palestine. To me this was always the core of the matter."[26]

Pearson played a central role in the final partition vote. Both the *New York Times* and *Manchester Guardian* ran articles about Pearson's role in the final stage of negotiations.[27] Dubbed the "Canadian plan" the final Subcommittee 1 agreement between the U.S. and USSR on how to implement partition was "a result of the tireless efforts of Lester B. Pearson," according to a front-page *New York Times* article.[28] Some Zionist groups called him "Lord Balfour" of Canada and "rabbi Pearson".[29] In 1960 Pearson received Israel's Medallion of Valour and after stepping down as prime minister in 1968, he received the Theodore Herzl award from the Zionist Organization of America for his "commitment to Jewish freedom and Israel."[30] The son of a minister, Pearson's Zionism was partly rooted in Christian teachings. His memoirs refer to Israel, "the land of my Sunday School lessons" where Pearson learned that "the Jews belonged in Palestine."[31] Above all else, Pearson, who was appointed external affairs minister a few months after facilitating Israel's creation, wanted to align himself and Canada with Washington, the world's emerging hegemon. "Pearson usually coordinated his moves with the Americans," one book on Canada's role in partition explained.[32] More than any other Canadian politician he was responsible for Canada's post-World War II shift away from British imperialism and towards the U.S. version. Pearson clearly sided with Washington during the Korean war, Suez crisis and Vietnam war. (See my *Black Book of Canadian Foreign Policy* for more detail.)

In *State in the Making,* David Horowitz, the first governor of the Bank of Israel and first director general of Israel's ministry of finance, writes: "The dynamic force and pathfinder was Lester Pearson. His adherence to the pro-partition fold was an important turning point. His influence, as one of the foremost figures at the UN was tremendous. It may be said that Canada more than any other country played a decisive part in all stages of the UNO discussions of Palestine. The activities at Lake Success of Lester Pearson and his fellow delegates were a fitting climax to Justice Rand's beneficent work on UNSCOP."[33]

By supporting partition Canadian officials opposed the indigenous population's moral and political claims to sovereignty over their territory.[34] Down from 90% at the start of the British mandate, by the end of 1947 Arabs still made up two-thirds of Palestine's population.[35] Despite making up only a third of the population, under the UN partition plan Jews received most of the territory. Ottawa supported a plan that gave the Zionist state

55% of Palestine despite the Jewish population owning less than seven per cent of the land.[36] Even "within the borders of their UN-proposed state, they [Jews] owned only eleven per cent of the land, and were the minority in every district. In the Negev [desert]…they constituted one per cent of the total population."[37]

Rand's assistant on UNSCOP, Leon Mayrand, provided a window into the dominant mindset at External Affairs. Most Palestinians were "incited by the menaces of a few feudal chiefs whose main interest is the maintenance of their privileges."[38] He believed that "The Arabs were bound to be vocal opponents of partition but they should not be taken too seriously. The great majority were not yet committed nationalists and the Arab chiefs could be appeased through financial concessions, especially if these accompanied a clearly declared will to impose a settlement whatever the means necessary."[39] A dissident within External Affairs and the Department's only Middle East expert, Elizabeth MacCallum, claimed Ottawa supported partition "because we didn't give two hoots for democracy."[40]

MacCallum's opinion wasn't popular with the ministry's power brokers. Pearson, for instance, organized late-night meetings allegedly to make it difficult for her to participate.[41] Despite failing to convince her superiors MacCallum displayed sharp foresight. At the time of partition, "MacCallum scribbled a note and passed it to Pearson saying the Middle East was now in for 'forty years' of war, due to the lack of consultation with the Arab countries."[42] She underestimated the duration of the conflict.

Far from being an "honest broker," Prime Minister St. Laurent admitted privately that Canada gained a reputation for "having taken up the Jewish cause."[43] The Canadian Jewish Congress echoed this statement claiming it was "heartwarming to Canadians to have history record that Canada played a most important part in the international deliberations which preceded this decision [on partition]."[44] Conversely, a representative from the Canadian Arab

Friendship League explained: "Canadian delegates, Mr. Lester B. Pearson and Mr. Justice C. Rand ... did their utmost to impose upon the Arabs the infamous partition scheme. The Arab world, I am sure, will remember them."[45]

Why did Canada push for partition? Some believe Ottawa supported Zionist aspirations under pressure from a Jewish lobby. Many Jewish Canadians, including prominent businessman Samuel Bronfman, did call for the creation of Israel. An organized Jewish Zionist lobby was active in Canada dating back to at least 1898 with the establishment of Montreal's Zionist Society.[46] The notion, however, that a Jewish Zionist lobby forced an unwilling Ottawa to support partition is exaggerated. Most accounts confirm that Jewish organizations were unable to convince government officials to lobby Great Britain to support Zionism. In late 1946, for instance, Zionists pressed Ottawa to "secure fuller sympathy in the United Kingdom for the proposals made by [U.S.] President Truman."[47] Ottawa ignored these calls. Similarly, the organized Jewish community was almost entirely unable to reverse Canada's anti-Semitic immigration policy in the preceding years, during and following the Second World War. Despite millions exterminated in Nazi concentration camps, Canada accepted fewer than 5,000 Jewish refugees from 1933 to 1945.[48]

Immediately after the Second World War, the Jewish community did not suddenly gain the necessary political clout to drive Canadian policy on Palestine. The way to understand Jewish Zionist lobbying is that it pressed against an almost open door. Together with Jewish lobbying, the anti-Semitism underlying Canada's "none is too many" policy towards Jewish refugees explains support for Israel. "Generally, the press supported the idea of Jewish emigration from Europe to Palestine after 1945, in large part, apparently, to forestall an influx of Jews to Canada."[49] After World War II there were a couple hundred thousand displaced Jews and Israel's creation lessened the pressure to accept them.[50] Pearson, for instance, believed sending these refugees to Palestine was the only sensible solution.[51] In February 1947, *Liberty Magazine* reported that "no spokesman will link Canada with Palestine but what everyone is going to know soon is that the displaced persons of Europe either come to Canada or go to Palestine. Politically it's a big question."[52]

Some Jewish Zionists even tapped into this anti-Semitism to advance their cause. "Fully cognizant of the government's reluctance to admit Jews to Canada, the [Zionist] delegation reminded [anti-Semitic Prime Minister Mackenzie] King that in the post war years, when 'multitudes of uprooted people ... would be knocking on the doors of all countries,' Palestine could accommodate many of the Jews who might want to come to Canada."[53]

Most displaced postwar refugees wanted to emigrate to Canada or the U.S. rather than Palestine where conflict was imminent. Despite the incineration of millions of European Jews they were refused entry. Instead, ships purchased in North America and manned by Canadians and Americans ferried some 33,000 Jewish refugees, about half the refugees that left Europe from mid-1946 until May 1948, to Palestine.[54]

The awful plight of post-WWII European Jewry gave Ottawa a reason for supporting Israel's creation. Yet, opponents of partition, especially after "the Canadian delegation explicitly refused a British proposal to have member states take Jewish refugees," were not fooled.[55] Pakistan's representative to the UN, Zafrullah Khan, explained: "Those who talk of humanitarian principles, and can afford to do most, have done the least at their own expense to alleviate [the Jewish refugee crisis]. But they are ready — indeed they are anxious — to be most generous at the expense of the Arab. Australia, Canada and the United States were opposed to returning the Jewish displaced persons to their countries of origin. But were they ready to absorb them themselves? Australia, an over-populated small country with congested areas, says no, no, no;

Canada, equally congested and over-populated, says no; the United States, a great humanitarian country, a small country, with small resources, says no. This was their contribution to the humanitarian principle, while stating at the same time: let them go to Palestine, where there are vast areas, a large economy and no trouble; they can easily be taken in there."[56]

World War II death camps helped justify Zionism. In the aftermath of Nazi atrocities many Jews previously opposed to Zionism's ethno-nationalistic character (understandably) changed their view. The brutality of European anti-Semitism, made more destructive by countries that refused to accept refugees, provided significant moral legitimacy to Zionism.

External Affairs knew it was hypocritical for Canada to support a Middle Eastern homeland as a way to make amends for European anti-Semitism. External Affairs dissident Elizabeth McCallum wrote: "Arabs regard it as a matter of essential justice that Europe itself should make reparation to the Jews for the sufferings it has inflicted on them. If the establishment of an independent Jewish state is regarded as the best permanent solution of the Jewish problem, the logical thing to do, they hold, is to force Germany to alienate territory for the purpose. If the United Nations hesitates to do this on the grounds that it would cause resentment and lead to future wars, precisely the same objection stands in the way of forcing the Arabs to alienate part of their patrimony — and in the latter case resentment would be increased by the knowledge that it was not the Arabs who had been responsible for the existence of a Jewish problem in Europe. If, on the contrary, Germany were merely asked to place a large fund at the disposal of the Jews, much of it to be used for the expansion of the Jewish National Home in Palestine, this again would mean that Arabs were being required to help pay for crimes they had not committed."[57]

More important than either the Jewish Zionist lobby or Jewish immigration, Canada's position on partition was driven by geopolitics. Most immediately, Ottawa was concerned with Anglo-American disunity over Palestine, more than the Palestinian crisis itself.[58] Canadian officials were concerned that disagreement between Washington and London over Palestine could adversely affect negotiations toward forming the North Atlantic Treaty Organization (NATO), which some say was a Canadian idea.[59]

By the mid-1940s Britain was under Arab pressure to reverse course and oppose the creation of Israel. Additionally, British officials were frustrated by the Zionist military offensive that weakened their position in the Middle East. But Ottawa's shift in imperial direction from London to Washington largely paralleled Zionism's changed patrons. During World War II Canada moved closer to Washington's growing sphere of influence so increasingly its perspective drove Canadian policy on Palestine. And the U.S. favoured a Jewish state.

To determine their position on the UN Ad Hoc Committee, for instance, Canada's delegation "found it especially important to know the American's position."[60] A member of the Canadian delegation explained: "[we] will have nothing to say until after the United States has spoken."[61]

Of central importance to Canadian support for partition was the belief that a Middle Eastern Jewish state would serve Western interests. Leading External Affairs mandarins Hume Wrong and Norman Robertson believed that "'if handled properly' the State of Israel could become a useful and friendly ally of the Western powers which would help resist Soviet penetration in the area."[62] An internal report circulated at External Affairs summarized Ottawa's thinking: "The plan of partition gives to the western powers the opportunity to establish an independent, progressive Jewish state in the Eastern Mediterranean with close economic and cultural ties with the West generally and in particular with the United States."[63] Ottawa largely supported Israel as a possible western outpost in the heart of the (oil-producing) Middle East.

Chapter 3
The ethnic cleansing of Palestine

The Canadian-backed UN partition of British Mandate Palestine contributed to the displacement of at least 700,000 Palestinians. Palestinian scholar Walid Khalidi complained that UN Resolution 181 was "a hasty act of granting half of Palestine to an ideological movement that declared openly already in the 1930s its wish to de-Arabise Palestine."[1] About half the "ethnically cleansed" Palestinians were forced from their homes between November 1947 and May 1948, before any Arab army entered Palestine.[2] A number of massacres that left hundreds of Palestinian civilians dead prompted the Arab countries to enter the conflict. Israeli historian Benny Morris explains: "The events [massacres] of April 1948 — Deir Yassin, Tiberias, Haifa, Jaffa — rattled and focused their [Arab governments] minds, and the arrival of tens of thousands of refugees drove home the urgency of direct intervention."[3]

Expelling more than 80% of the Palestinian population was an imperative for the Zionist leadership because they wanted a homogenous Jewish state. Without the forcible displacement of the Palestinians, Jews would have been only half the population in the UN designated Jewish state.[4]

Canadians, with some direct support from Ottawa, supported efforts to de-Arabize Palestine. Canadians such as Dov Yosef — the former head of Canadian Young Judea — participated in the Jewish Agency's Population Transfer Committee, which called for the expulsion of Arab Palestinians.[5] More concretely, "Canadian radio sets and other radio equipment became the backbone of Israel's military communications network" in 1948.[6] The Purchasing Commission of the United Zionist Council, the umbrella organization of Canadian Zionism, bought weapons and other materials for the war effort.[7] "Canadians smuggled military equipment, including machine gun parts, to Haganah forces in Palestine; sometimes this simply involved misnaming cargo shipments: 'Flame throwers became insecticide sprayers.'"[8] The most blatantly contraband products were sent via dummy companies "Victory Equipment" and "Supply Limited".[9]

Even though Ottawa caught wind of these arms exports no Canadian was ever charged with illegally exporting arms.[10] Worse still, some government officials (quietly) supported weapons exports to Palestine. In his biography Edgar Bronfman reports, "Father [Samuel Bronfman], too, was a Zionist, and had been very active in the securing of arms for the Israelis during Israel's War of Independence in 1948: I overheard conversations of his with various Canadian government officials persuading them to sell them arms."[11] Alex Skelton, a functionary at Trade and Commerce and son of former Deputy Minister of External Affairs O. D. Skelton, arranged export permits to Palestine for numerous militarily useful items.[12] Skelton came up with the idea of sending airplanes to a non-existent "Tel Aviv Spring Fair" — created to justify exporting single engine Harvard trainer monoplanes that were easily convertible to military uses.[13]

A number of Canadians, with at least tacit support from Ottawa, played a direct role in de-Arabising Palestine. Representatives from Haganah, the primary Zionist military force, recruited 300 experienced Canadian soldiers to serve in Israel's ranks during the war unleashed by partition and Zionist ethnic cleansing.[14] The heir to Tiptop Tailors, Ben Dunkelman, Haganah's main recruiter in Canada, claimed "about one thousand" Canadians "fought to establish Israel."[15] More than half a million dollars was raised to pay for the travel and living costs of the Canadian troops.[16]

During the 1948 war Israel's small air force was almost entirely foreign, with at least 53 Canadians, including 15 non-Jews, enlisted.[17] Additionally, a number of top-notch American pilots were recruited by a Windsor, Ont., native who toured the U.S. Midwest to build the Zionist air force.[18]

"The most decorated Jewish serviceman in Canada", Montreal's Sydney Shulemson, is considered the "father of the Israeli Air Force."[19] Another Canadian commanded the Zionist's central airbase, Sde Dov.[20] Drawing wide media attention, Canada's top World War II fighter ace went to fight for Israel.[21] There is some disagreement on why Buzz Beurling, who died en route to Israel, was willing to fight. Some claim he was paid a large sum, citing the role of leading Montreal capitalist, "[Samuel] Bronfman [who] personally underwrote life insurance policies for the Canadian pilots recruited to help Israel fight its 1948 War of Independence."[22] Others say Beurling was motivated by religion. A devout Christian, Beurling rarely swore or drank. "I would be helping to fulfill prophecies and teachings of the Bible," he explained.[23]

Canadian pilots played an important role in the limited air campaign. "World War II RCAF [Royal Canadian Air Force] veteran Clifford Denzel (Denny) Wilson of Hamilton, Ont., shot down two Egyptian Spitfires, while Joseph John Doyle and John McElroy of London [Ont.] downed three and four Arab aircraft, respectively, while Flying Officer Leonard Fitchett was killed during a bomber attack on an Egyptian-held fortress."[24] In January 1949 four unarmed British Spitfires, trying to find out if Israeli troops were still in Egypt, were shot down over Egyptian territory by an American and Canadian (both non-Jewish) pilot.[25] An always-boastful Dunkelman claimed that "Canadian pilots accounted for one-third of all Arab planes shot down in that war."[26]

Almost all the volunteers were veterans of the Canadian Armed Forces.[27] A World War II veteran of the Royal Canadian Air Force and Royal Canadian Army, Ben Ocopnick served in Israel's Army, Navy and Air Force.[28] Israel's first tank commander, Lionel Druker, was also a World War II veteran from Sydney, Nova Scotia.[29]

Dunkelman writes that "the Hagana command had decided to recruit experienced combat soldiers to serve in the Jewish forces.

They wanted me to get to work on recruiting an infantry brigade of English-speaking volunteers, which I would lead in action."[30] Hagana's 52nd Battalion had a Canadian platoon.[31]

Ottawa did little to stop Canadians from joining Israel's fight despite outlawing recruitment for a foreign army during the Spanish Civil War.[32] Far from stopping it, Canadian diplomacy helped gain the release of Canadians detained in Lebanon en route to fight in Palestine.[33]

Tired of recruiting others, Dunkelman left for Palestine to put his Canadian acquired military skills — he was particularly adept with mortars — at the service of the Zionist project. "By the summer of 1948, he [Dunkelman] was in command of a Brigade actively depopulating Palestinian villages by force — a unit so heavily comprised of recruits from Canada, the United States and South Africa that it came to be known as the 'Anglo-Saxon Brigade.'"[34]

Operating in the Arab dominated northern part of current day Israel the Dunkelman-led troops were particularly brutal. "In many of the Palestinian oral histories that have now come to the fore," Ilan Pappé notes, "few brigade names appear. However, [Dunkelman's] Brigade Seven is mentioned again and again, together with such adjectives as 'terrorists' and 'barbarous.'"[35]

The Seventh Brigade carried out atrocities in Safsaf, Saliha, Sa'sa and Jish.[36] Between 60 and 94 Palestinians were killed in Saliha, a northern town of a couple thousand.[37] A Jewish National Fund official, Yosef Nahmani, noted in his diary that "60-70" men and women were killed after they "had raised a white flag."[38]

In Jish, a local politician recounted: "the [Dunkelman-led] army surrounded the village and carried out searches. In the course of the search soldiers robbed several of the houses and stole 605 pounds, jewelry and other valuables. When the people who were robbed insisted on being given receipts for their property, they were taken to a remote place and shot dead."[39]

While he doesn't take responsibility for any massacres in his biography, Dunkelman makes some surprising admissions. "In flagrant defiance of the law," Dunkelman boasted, "we undertook many trips across the Lebanese border."[40] In another instance Dunkelman writes about the Seventh Brigade's collaboration with the Druze in the town of Shafa Amr. "Everything went according to plan. While the Moslem section [of town] was being shelled, the assault force — the 79th Armoured Battalion under Joe Weiner ["a former permanent force sergeant-major in the Canadian artillery who had been with me in the mortars"], with two companies from Arele Yariv's 21st Battalion — approached the walls. They and the Druze defenders fired harmlessly over each other's heads. The attackers quietly passed through the Druze lines, entering the village and taking the Moslems from the rear. Within a short time, the whole village was securely in our hands."[41]

In Israel Dunkelman was celebrated with a bridge on the Lebanese border called Gesher Ben.[42] The Canadian press also cheered his actions. Dunkelman "helped in the liberation of northern Israel," the *Toronto Star* reported in 1997.[43] In 1999 the *Globe and Mail* added that Dunkelman was "a Canadian and Israeli war hero."[44]

A major aim of the 47/48 war was to rid the state of its indigenous inhabitants and then to take their land. Of the 20,418,023 dunums of land held by the Israeli state at the end of the war only 1,475,766 were owned by Jews.[45] So, Palestinian refugees were not allowed to reclaim their property. The 1950 Knesset Absentee Property Law declared lands "abandoned" if the owner or owners were absent for even one day after November 1947. This was designed "to justify the taking of Arab lands and buildings for the sake of consolidating Israel's hold on the bulk of the land area."[46] One group particularly victimized by this law were, and are, "present absentees" (or internally displaced Palestinians), which includes 274,000 current day Arab citizens of Israel.[47] "Present absentees are not permitted to live in the homes they were expelled from, even if they live in the same area, the property still exists, and they can show that they own it. They are regarded as absent by the Israeli government because they left their homes, even if they did not intend to leave them for more than a few days, and even if they did so involuntarily."[48]

Not satisfied with taking the property of the Palestinian population living within the UN-defined Jewish state, during the 1948 war Israel grabbed 24% more land than it was allotted by the UN's (already unjust) Resolution 181.[49] On November 4, 1948 the British, Chinese and Americans supported a resolution to force Israel to withdraw from territory it captured beyond the UN partition plan and to impose sanctions if it refused. "Pearson was surprised; he had believed the U.S. would not back anything that included the threat of sanctions, and tried to convince the council to postpone action until Friday Five November, so that he could find out what the Americans were up to. The British and Americans would have none of this, however, and lobbied strongly for passage. Pearson resented their haste and tried not to be 'indecently rushed' but there was little he could do. At the evening session the resolution was adopted. Pearson voted for, but he strongly resisted a Lebanese and British effort to have it apply to Galilee as well the Negev."[50]

More generally, Pearson dismissed Arab claims that Israel enlarged her territory illegally — beyond the UN partition plan.[51] In November 1948, Pearson told the General Assembly, "we must deal with the fact that a Jewish state has come into existence and has established its control over territory from which it will not be dislodged and we must address ourselves to the problem of regulating the relations of this community with its neighbors. I do not deny for a moment that this is a difficult circumstance for the Arab states to accept, but it is nevertheless the case."[52]

Despite working on the (generous) partition plan, after the 1948 war Pearson changed tack. His proposals left Israel in control of its territorial gains with no mention of the Palestinian state as per the partition plan.[53] Similarly, when Israel proclaimed Jerusalem its capital in December 1949 Canada failed to advocate that it be put under international control, which was called for in the 1947 partition plan. In December 1949 the General Assembly voted 38 to 14 in support of an Australian resolution calling for the internationalization of Jerusalem. Canada voted no.[54]

Chapter 4
Decades of one-sided support

Canada's active support of one side in the Israel-Palestine conflict continued after the State of Israel became a reality. Between 1950 and 1956 Ottawa sold Israel a significant amount of weapons. At the National Archives there is a 150-page thesis detailing Canadian weapons sales to Israel from the state's founding until its invasion of Egypt in 1956. "By the summer of 1950," the author notes, "Israeli arms requests were being placed in Canada with an almost regular frequency, and from this point until the 1956 Suez war, there was never a time when a substantial Israeli arms request was not under consideration by the Canadian government."[1]

These weapon sales did not go unnoticed. "Canada and a few other nations were named by [Egyptian President Abdul] Nasser as being Israel's military suppliers, guilty of strengthening Egypt's great enemy."[2] Canada continued to arm Israel even after the Israel Defence Force (IDF) launched a number of murderous raids into Gaza and Egypt that left dozens of soldiers and civilians dead in 1954 and 1955.[3]

Under U.S. pressure Ottawa agreed to sell twenty-four F86 jets to Israel in early 1956. Washington didn't want to openly back Israel so they asked Ottawa to sell the advanced fighter jets.[4] Assistant Under-Secretary of State for External Affairs R. M. MacDonnell privately argued that Ottawa, unlike Washington, could send jets to Israel without suffering a major backlash. According to MacDonnell, Canada had limited direct economic or political interests in the region and would at most "suffer a few broken windows in our missions in Cairo and Beirut."[5]

Once Ottawa decided to sell jets to Israel the Prime Minister's Office explained: "After full and useful discussion with certain friendly governments, the Canadian government has now decided that it would not be justified in refusing a request made some time ago by the government of Israel for permission to purchase interceptor planes from Canadian production for use in the defence of that country. The government has been greatly influenced in this decision by the fact that Israel's neighbor has recently received... from the Soviet Union... a considerable number of modern jet fighters, of which Israel possesses none. Assurances have been received from the government of Israel that interceptors in question will be used solely for defence against aggression."[6]

In September 1956 Nasser condemned Ottawa for selling Israel F86 jets. "The supplying of Israel with arms despite her repeated aggressions against Arab frontiers is considered a hostile act aimed at the whole Arab nation."[7]

Israel used Canadian-acquired weapons when it invaded Egypt in 1956. On top of the weapons sales, Canadian pronouncements in the lead up to the Israeli invasion were decidely anti-Egypt. Even though the investors were fully compensated, External Affairs Minister Lester Pearson criticized Nasser's July 1956 nationalization of the Suez Canal Company, which precipitated the invasion. Pearson complained: "The violation by the government of Egypt of an international convention governing the use of an international waterway so important as the Suez Canal is, of course, to be condemned. Possibly it should be recalled at this time that the convention in question attempted to safeguard the free use of the waterway in war and peace. In that sense, the convention was already violated by the Egyptian government when the Israeli vessels were prevented from using the canal."[8]

Despite criticizing the nationalization of the canal and selling Israel weapons, Ottawa opposed that country's 1956 invasion of Egypt. During that invasion Israel conspired with the region's fading imperial powers, Britain and France, against the wishes of the emerging power, Washington. The U.S. opposed the western invasion, fearing it would add to Soviet prestige in a geo-strategically important region. American powerbrokers also wanted the former imperial powers to understand that there was a new master in the region. Ottawa sided with Washington. After coordinating with U.S. Secretary of State John Foster Dulles, Pearson proposed a UN peacekeeping mission to separate the warring factions. Ottawa was primarily concerned about the disagreement between the U.S. and U.K. over the intervention, not Egyptian sovereignty or the plight of that country's population. Pearson proposed placing the United Nations Emergency Force (UNEF) on Egyptian soil. He never made a serious push to station any UN troops on the territory of the aggressor. "Israel would not accept foreign troops upon her soil," explained Prime Minister Ben-Gurion.[9]

The Suez crisis created a rift between Canada and Israel, but it was shortlived. Pearson later summarized Canada's position vis-à-vis Israel. "We worked as hard as we possibly could with the Americans to get their support for a resolution which would lay down in detail specifically the arrangements we should follow for the withdrawal of foreign troops and Israeli troops from Egypt. We weren't successful. We did our best to modify their attitude. We also told them, and in no uncertain terms, that if they supported a resolution of sanctions against Israel, we would have to break with them because we would not support it in those circumstances."[10]

Pearson pressed Israel to remove its troops from Egypt but he did so with the country's interests in mind. After France and England pulled out, he told Israeli officials to withdraw or "you run the risk of losing all your friends."[11] In his memoirs, Pearson called Israel's invasion "a defensive action to protect themselves."[12]

Opposed by the Arab countries, India and many other former colonies, Pearson saw UNEF largely as an occupation force.[13] Eight months into the UN mission, Pearson explained: "We feel that Egypt had the right to be consulted and to agree to the entry of an international force, but having given that consent as she did, she has no right to control the force, to order it about, to tell the force when it shall leave. If Egypt is dissatisfied with the operation of the force, or if anybody else is dissatisfied, or if Egypt wants the force to withdraw, feels its work is completed, Egypt should make its views known to the Secretary-General who would take it up with the Committee of Seven [of which Pearson was a member] and then it would go to the full assembly, and until the assembly had decided the force would carry on."[14]

Israel's view of UNEF was similar. Israel believed UNEF "cannot be subordinated to Egypt's desires. Its movements and its composition cannot be the subject of dictation by the host country."[15]

Pearson's bias against Egypt was also on display regarding the Gaza strip. He wanted to take Gaza away from Egyptian administration and make it UN controlled. Pearson called for the UN to "accept responsibility to the maximum possible extent for establishing and maintaining effective civil administration in the Gaza Strip."[16] This proposal was rejected by the Arab countries because it would've made it more difficult to expose Israeli aggression on Palestine. Syria's spokesperson at the UN said, "The representative of Canada is trying to show various faces in various directions. Canada is deftly supporting the Zionist policy."[17] For his part, Jordan's representative reminded the General Assembly that Pearson played an important role in the partition plan that created a Jewish state on Palestinian land.[18]

More than a decade after arriving, UN troops were expelled from Egypt. On May 28, 1967, Canada's 800-man contingent was ordered to leave the country within 48 hours. In the lead up to Israel's June 1967 invasion of Egypt, Canada co-sponsored (with Denmark) an emergency Security Council meeting to call attention to Egypt's blockade of Israeli shipping through the Strait of Tiran on the Gulf of Aqaba. Ottawa made this move while Secretary General U Thant negotiated the issue with Nasser in Cairo.[19] The emergency meeting contributed to the sense of crisis, which Israel used to justify invading Egypt.[20] Ottawa also supported a British and American proposal to establish a maritime force to protect Israeli shipping. On May 26, 1967, Prime Minister Pearson told the House of Commons that he and President Lyndon B. Johnson were "in complete agreement" on the "importance of maintaining the right of access to an innocent passage through the Gulf of Aqaba, and everything possible should be done through the UN to see if this can be arranged."[21] Made during a politically turbulent time, the Egyptians considered Ottawa's actions a threat. This prompted Nasser to expel Canadian troops. In response to Canada's aggressive posture, public protests took place at the Canadian Chancellery building in Egypt.[22] Al Ahram newspaper wrote that Canada was "a stooge of the Western powers who seek to colonize the Arab world with Israel's help."[23] For his part, Nasser complained about Ottawa's "biased stand in favour of Israel."[24]

Canada, Britain and the U.S. exaggerated the importance of Egypt's blockade of Israeli shipping through the Strait of Tiran. Iranian oil shipments were the only important commodity affected by the blockade and they could have been rerouted to Haifa.[25] More generally, Harvard Law Professor Roger Fisher explains: "The United Arab Republic [Egypt] had a good legal case for restricting traffic through the Straits of Tiran. First, it is debatable whether international law confers any rights of innocent passage through such a waterway. Despite an Israeli request, the International Law Commission in 1956 found no rule which would govern the Straits of Tiran. Although the 1958 convention on the Territorial Sea does provide for innocent passage through such straits, the United States Representative, Arthur Dean, called this 'a new rule' and U.A.R. has not signed the treaty. There are, of course, good arguments on the Israeli side too, and an impartial international court might well conclude that the right of innocent passage through the Straits of Tiran does exist. But a right of innocent passage is not a right of free passage for any cargo at any time. In the words of the convention on the Territorial Sea: 'passage is innocent so long as it is not prejudicial to the peace, good order or security of the coastal states.' In April Israel conducted major retaliatory raids on Syria and threatened raids of still greater size. In this situation was Egypt required by international law to continue to allow Israel to bring oil and other strategic supplies through Egyptian territory — supplies which Israel could use to conduct further military raids? That was the critical question of law."[26]

Egypt's blockade of Israeli shipping garnered greater attention than it deserved while Israel's geostrategic aims were downplayed. According to a CIA analysis just before the June 1967 war, Israel's goals were (1) "Destruction of the center of power of the radical Arab Socialist movement, i.e. the Nasser regime." (2) "Destruction of the arms of the radical Arabs." (3) "Destruction of both Syria and Jordan as modern states."[27]

Alongside Washington, Ottawa apparently supported these objectives. Ignoring Israeli belligerance, during the war Pearson told the House "the basic issue in this situation, it seems to me, as has already been mentioned in this debate, is the recognition of Israel's right to live in peace and security. So long as Israel's neighbors, or some of them, refused to recognize the right of Israel to exist, then we move from one crisis to another. Israel, of course, also has the basic obligation, which I am sure she accepts, to live without provocations and threats to her neighbors and in accord with United Nations' resolutions which gave her birth."[28]

Canada continued to defend Israeli policy after it won the war. Even after Israel won the war in six days Pearson implied that Israel faced an Arab Goliath. Pearson said "Israel is quite entitled to receive from the international community a greater guarantee of her security than she has had in the past."[29] On June 12 Prime Minister Levi Eshkol said Israel would decide the fruits of its 1967 victory. The next day, Pearson said Ottawa would oppose a UN resolution if it was "merely in terms which denounce Israel as an aggressor in this particular matter within the meaning of the charter."[30]

Following through on Pearson's statement, Canada voted against a Yugoslav resolution calling for Israel to withdraw behind the armistice lines and for the Secretary-General to consider remaining questions immediately after Israel's withdrawal.[31] Ali Dessouki explains: "Canada has to recognize the inconsistency between its policy in May prior to the hostilities, and its policy after the Israeli victory. Prior to the hostilities, Canada's view was that no progress in negotiations could take place unless the Gulf of Aqaba were reopened to Israeli shipping thereby restoring the status quo ante. Following the Israeli victory Canada adopted an entirely different position. Now, restoration of the status quo, i.e., withdrawal of Israeli forces together with international guarantees of Israeli shipping rights, must be accompanied by a political settlement of all major issues."[32]

Ottawa actively supported Israel before, during and after the 1967 war. During that war between 200,000 and 250,000 Palestinians were expelled from the West Bank (17,000 were allowed to return) and three months after the conclusion of hostilites Israel began setting up illegal settlements.[33] The 1967 war led to Israel's four decade-long occupation of the West Bank, Gaza and Golan Heights.

In May 1968 the Security Council called on Israel to drop its plan to annex East Jerusalem, which it captured during the war. Except for Ottawa and Washington's abstentions the vote was unanimous.[34] "[External Affairs Minister Paul] Martin apparently accepted Israel's unilateral annexation of the city. According to the *Canadian Jewish News*, Mr. Martin sent its editor a statement in which he declared, 'no one expects Israel to leave united Jerusalem.'"[35]

Throughout the 1950s and 60s Ottawa joined Washington and most other Western countries, which then dominated the General Assembly, in opposing resolutions critical of Israel. In a study of Canada's voting pattern Jack Zubrzycki explained: "In

1947, Palestinians were recognized as a 'people' with a distinct national consciousness; by the 1960s, the government viewed them as refugees, requiring humanitarian aid, and the Canadian government submerged conceptions of Palestinian consciousness within an Arab identity. This meant that the Canadian government treated Palestinian claims of self-determination as illegitimate or weak; since it was not considered a national problem to be solved politically, humanitarian aid was deemed sufficient. At best, Canada supported individual Palestinian rights, not collective rights. Between 1969 and 1972, for example, Canada voted against four General Assembly resolutions recognizing Palestinian 'rights.' One rationale is particularly indicative of Canada's priorities, as one senior DEA [Department of External Affairs] official stated 'that [Minister of External Affairs Mitchell] Mr. Sharp was absent from Ottawa at the time of the vote on some Middle Eastern issues in 1972. When contacted, his instructions were to find out how the U.S. was voting and do likewise.' Only during the 1974 - 1976 period, when Canada agreed to Palestinian representation at prospective peace settlements, was there even a symbolic recognition of Palestinian collective rights. Even this was not necessarily a step forward, since Canada's continued support for an Israeli 'veto' power in determining Palestinian representatives undermined any potential substance to Palestinian self-determination of representatives."[36]

In the early 1970s Ottawa extended a $126 million Export Development Corporation line of credit to Israel and, as is still the case today, opposed the main political force working to counter Israel's claims towards the West Bank and Gaza.[37] Canada was one of only a handful of countries that voted against a 1974 General Assembly resolution affirming the Palestinian Liberation Organization's (PLO) right "to participate on equal footing, in all UN deliberations in the Middle East."[38] Secretary of State for External Affairs Alan J. MacEachen told the General Assembly: "The claim of the Palestine Liberation Organization to represent the Palestinians is ... not for Canada to decide. It is a question that remains to be resolved by the parties directly involved in the course of their continuing efforts to work towards an agreed peace, and Israel, in our view, is an essential party in deciding the question."[39] A week after the UN voted to accept PLO participation, Conservative and Liberal MPs agreed that Israel needed to okay the PLO's participation at a UN conference.[40]

Ottawa took the same line a couple years later. External Affairs Minister MacEachen explained: "Israel must have some involvement in the selection of the group or individual who speaks for the Palestinians in peace talks. There would be little prospect of settlement or negotiation unless Israel recognizes the Palestinian representatives."[41]

In one of the most contentious and far-reaching votes since partition, in November 1975 the General Assembly called Zionism a form of racism. The resolution passed 72 to 35 with 35 abstentions. Ottawa strongly objected even though non-Jews in Israel are clearly second class citizens. A day after the Zionism equals racism resolution passed, the House of Commons unanimously condemned it.[42] "Canada has opposed on all occasions any equation of Zionism and racism, whether stated directly or implied indirectly in resolutions."[43] For years Ottawa pushed to rescind this resolution. Their efforts bore fruit in December 1991.

In the early 1980s Ottawa sided with Israel on a spate of UN resolutions despite near unanimity of international opposition. In late July 1980 Canada voted with the U.S. and Israel (nine European countries abstained) against a resolution calling on Israel to withdraw completely and unconditionally from all Palestinian and Arab territories occupied since 1967.[44] Days later Ottawa voted with Israel and Washington against criticism of Israel at a UN conference in Copenhagen.[45] Six months thereafter Ottawa found itself a bit less isolated in defence of Israeli conduct. Australia joined Canada and the U.S. in opposition to a resolution that mentioned "the arming of settlers ... to commit acts of violence against Arab civilians, mass arrests, and collective punishment."[46] On December 11, 1982 the *Globe and Mail* reported that the "United Nations General Assembly called yesterday for the creation of an independent Palestinian state and for Israel's unconditional withdrawal from territories it occupied in 1967. Israel, Canada, the United States and Costa Rica cast the only negative votes as the assembly passed the appeal by 113 votes to 4, with 23 abstentions."[47] Six months later a *Globe and Mail* article referred to "Canada's position as Israel's No. 2 friend at the UN."[48]

During the 1980s Ottawa tacitly supported Israeli aggression in the region. In June 1981 Israel, an atomic power, bombed the Osiraq nuclear reactor near Baghdad. Fifty-one UN members voted to condemn Israel's action while eight countries refused to criticize the bombing (the U.S. was the only Western country to vote no). Twenty-seven countries abstained, including Canada.[49] Six weeks later Canada opposed a call for Israel to be expelled from the International Atomic Energy Agency for bombing Iraq.[50]

The next year the Israeli army tried to go all the way to Beirut in a bid to destroy the PLO and to install a client government.[51] Unlike Harper in 2006, Pierre Trudeau at least publicly criticized Israel's 1982 invasion of Lebanon. But this opposition was at best symbolic. "As a result of strong pro-Israel bias in the cabinet, the government was unable to take any unequivocal public position on the invasion of Lebanon or the massacre of Palestinian refugees in the Sabra and Chatila refugee camps in September 1982."[52] During the 15th and 16th of September 1982, Israeli backed right-wing Christian militias slaughtered as many as 2,000 defenceless Palestinian civilians at the Sabra and Shatila refugee camp.[53] The House of Commons failed to unanimously support a resolution pronouncing "its disgust for those forces that were responsible for the slaughter and urge upon them a policy of restraint."[54] Only months after the Sabra and Shatila massacre Israeli Defence Minister

Ariel Sharon, who was later judged indirectly responsible for the slaughter, visited Canada. Despite protests, Liberal MPs, including future ambassador to Tel Aviv David Berger, enthusiastically defended Sharon's visit.[55]

Ottawa failed to unequivocally condemn Israel's invasion, let alone impose sanctions as it did when the Soviet Union invaded Afghanistan three years earlier or during Argentina's invasion of the Falkland Islands the same year. Canada "is not considering sanctions against Israel such as those imposed against Argentina after it invaded the Falkland Islands," noted External Affairs Minister Mark MacGuigan.[56] "The Argentinians were acting by force to take permanently territory to which they laid claim. While we do not approve of Israel's actions and regard them as being in violation of international law, they are not laying any kind of sovereign claim to this territory and indeed they have now agreed to a cease-fire."[57]

Israel occupied southern Lebanon for 18 years and would likely still be there if it were not for Hezbollah's tenacious resistance. Instead of imposing sanctions (diplomatic or economic) for its 18-year occupation of Lebanon, during the 1980s Export Development Canada (EDC) provided tens of millions of dollars in credits to Israel.[58] Ottawa continued business as usual with Israel.

As Israel suppressed the Palestinian resistance and occupied Lebanon, Canadian diplomatic support for Israel was strong. A 1987 survey of UN members ranked Canada second to the U.S. in perceived support for Israel.[59] Canadian diplomats echoed this pro-Israeli perception. A study of former ambassadors and diplomats in the late 1980s found that the vast majority felt Canada's relations were "unbalanced" with respect to Israel in Middle East peace negotiations. None of the ambassadors felt Canada was unbalanced in the Palestinians favor.[60] In the early 1990s noted critic of Israel Norman Finkelstein argued that "Canada, [is] probably Israel's staunchest ally after the United States at the United Nations."[61]

Begun in late 1993 the Oslo peace negotiations dampened the conflict. Many countries initiated or expanded diplomatic and economic relations with Israel during this period. Unfortunately, the "peace process" was little more than an Israeli/Washington charade to get the Yasir Arafat-led Palestinian Authority to oversee the occupation. While the PA suppressed resistance to the occupation Israel continued its colonization of Palestinian lands. During seven years of peace negotiations 80,000 Israelis settled in the West Bank and East Jerusalem.[62]

Following Washington's lead, Ottawa helped shape the geopolitical landscape to better serve Israel. Relations with Egypt improved in the early 1980s partly because that country signed the 1979 Camp David peace accord with Israel. Following on the heels of the Egypt-U.S. business council, which was established after the U.S.-brokered peace agreement, 35 major Canadian companies (Bell Canada, Dome Petroleum, General Motors of Canada etc.) visited Egypt in late 1981.[63] At the same time the federal government began a major aid program for Egypt. The EDC provided a $55.2-million (U.S.) loan to help finance the Shoubrah El-Kheima power project while the Canadian International Development Agency (CIDA) chipped in with a $12.5-million (Cdn.) loan and a $7.5-million grant.[64] Into the early 1990s "most of Canada's modest aid to the Middle East ... [went] to Egypt."[65]

By further undermining secular Arab nationalism and increasing Washington's military presence in the Middle East, the 1991 attack on Iraq strenghtened Israel's regional position. Along with the U.S., U.K., France and Italy, Canada contributed significantly to the war effort. Ottawa dispatched two destroyers and a supply vessel, 24 CF-18 attack jets and 1,700 ground troops.[66] Canada was among a handful of coalition members to engage its forces in combat.[67]

To undercut Arab support for the U.S.-led invasion and to draw attention to the war's wider geopolitical aims, Baghdad fired 39 SCUD missiles into Israel.[68] Israeli leaders were warned about incoming SCUDs by the Canada/U.S. operated NORAD/ USSPACECOM missile-warning Center at Cheyenne Mountain Colorado.[69] (In a sign of North American support for Israel, NORAD was put on high alert during the October 1973 (Yom Kippur) war.)

Some commentators claim Ottawa took a more aggressive posture towards Iraq after it bombed Israel. Whether or not this was the case it was definetely used to justify Canadian military engagement to an antiwar public. Immediately after the first SCUDs were fired Prime Minister Brian Mulroney said: "Canada will not sit idly in the face of unprovoked attacks [on Israel] ... We will commit a full and, if need be, a growing role."[70] Barely a day after the first Iraqi missiles fell on Israel, Canadian fighters began sweep-and-escort missions alongside American jets bombing Iraq. Four days later Mulroney told the House of Commons: "We have resolved never to remain indifferent while Israel is threatened with mass destruction."[71]

Chapter 5
Ties that bind — intelligence, military and business

Canada is more than simply a friend and ally to Israel in the diplomatic arena. In every other aspect of foreign policy Canada is not and never has been an honest broker in the Israel/Palestine conflict. In fact, one could argue that Canada has never honestly considered the merits of any position other than being an outright advocate of Israel. The following two chapters describe various aspects of Canada's broader policy in the Middle East.

Intelligence

Intelligence services are an important component of a country's foreign policy. Canadian security services have sided and continue to side with Israel. While intelligence agencies are highly secretive, by all indications the Canadian Security Intelligence Service (CSIS) works closely with its Israeli counterpart, Mossad. CSIS trades "information with friendly foreign intelligence services such as American or Israeli."[1] One book about spies explains: "Israel's very effective spy agency, Mossad, and CSIS have close relationships in countering terrorists."[2] Canada's ambassador to Tel Aviv from 1992 to 1995 concurs. Norman Spector, who said there was a CSIS operative working for him at the embassy, referred to the "very close cooperation" between the Canadian and Israeli spy agencies.[3]

Reportedly, CSIS and Mossad work together inside Canada. "Mossad agents are located in every major [Canadian] city, working closely with CSIS, to protect El Al aircraft and airline installations and watching PLO political activities, especially those of Arab and Iranian students. Israelis are CSIS's prime source of information on a number of suspected terrorists and spies, but often the information is laundered through Washington."[4] For his part, Spector claimed Mossad shared information with CSIS on potential

Arab immigrants. "Most of the information provided by Israel is routine, although it can be very helpful in rooting out terrorists and other undesirable elements who wish to take advantage of Canada's liberal immigration policies."[5]

During the mid-1990s peace negotiations many Palestinian Canadians accused CSIS of intimidating opponents of the peace deal. The Canadian spy agency allegedly offered cash in exchange for information on those opposed to the PLO's compromise, which divided the West Bank into three cantons cut off from each other by Israeli bypass roads.[6] "CSIS is carrying out a political agenda by targeting only those who are aligned with non-Fatah groups of the PLO — those who oppose the [Oslo peace] accord signed by the PLO. More than 20 PFLP [Popular Front for the Liberation of Palestine] supporters have come forward alleging that they have been interrogated by CSIS."[7] Reg Whitaker, an expert on CSIS, argued that: "There are reasonable grounds to suspect that both groups [the PFLP and the Democratic Front for the Liberation of Palestine] are on some sort of blacklist involving Western countries."[8]

After 9/11 blacklists took on an official character and numerous Palestinian groups were branded terrorists, including the PFLP.[9] "The Canadian government has criminalized nearly all major Palestinian political parties by designating them 'terrorist groups' under Bill C-36," which makes it illegal to support such groups in any way.[10] In March 2009 Ottawa even barred British MP George Galloway from Canada for delivering humanitarian aid to Hamas officials who were the democratically elected administration in the Gaza strip.

The capacity to designate individuals "supporters of terrorism" provides intelligence agencies with a powerful tool to intimidate. CSIS has also been accused of telling Palestinians that if they do not cooperate they will be turned over to Mossad, which is known for using brutal interrogation methods.[11] Fearful of Mossad or other consequences, some Palestinians help CSIS. This information often finds its way to Mossad. *Spy Wars* describes how CSIS "told him [an unnamed Palestinian] explicitly they were gathering information for the CIA and Mossad."[12]

CSIS is not the only arm of the federal government that gathers intelligence for Israel. Based in Canadian embassies around the world, the Communications Security Establishment is known to have spied on Palestinian activists for decades.[13] "Yasser Arafat's name, for instance, was on every [Communications Security Establishment] key word list. [Washington's] NSA [National Security Agency] was happy about that."[14]

According to Norman Spector, Mossad's relationship to CSIS "goes beyond information sharing. There are joint operations."[15] Legally bound to secrecy, Spector was not in a position to provide much detail, but it is public knowledge that Mossad agents have used Canadian passports to carry out numerous foreign assassinations. "A member of an Israeli hit squad that mistakenly killed a Moroccan waiter in Norway in 1973 had posed as a Canadian," reported the *Canadian Jewish News*.[16] In 1974 some 50 blank Canadian passports disappeared from a vault at the Canadian Embassy in Vienna. The next year a Mossad team in Cyprus was seized "after a hotel bombing in which a Palestinian guerrilla leader was killed. The passport used by one of the Israeli hitmen had a number that revealed it to be from among the 50 stolen in Vienna."[17]

After the Norway and Cyprus incidents Israel promised to stop using Canadian cover when assassinating Palestinians (or others) abroad.[18] Despite Israel's assurances, Victor Ostrovsky said he saw "more than a thousand" blank Canadian passports in a Mossad forgery factory in Israel. A Mossad agent in the mid 1980s, Ostrovsky claimed Canadian passports are "still the favorite of the Mossad."[19]

Until 1997 Israeli agents' use of Canadian cover received little attention. That changed when Prime Minister Benjamin

Netanyahu responded to a Hamas offer for a 30-year truce (relayed by Jordan's King Hussein) by trying to kill the group's Jordanian branch chief, Khalid Meshal.[20] The Israeli agents, who were captured after dropping poison in Meshal's ear, entered Jordan on Canadian passports.[21] King Hussein responded angrily to this attack against Jordan's sovereignty, forcing Israel to provide the antidote for the poison. (Despite widespread domestic opposition, Hussein had signed a peace accord with Israel three years earlier.) Widely covered by the media, the hit helped undermine Netanyahu's first government. Foreign Affairs Minister Lloyd Axworthy initially responded gingerly to the assassination attempt. For the first "week Canadian authorities said nothing about the affair, other than to repeat the rather incredible story that two Canadian tourists had attacked a Hamas leader."[22] Once the real story began to emerge, Spector notes, "Axworthy finally changed tack, adopting a tone of great umbrage."[23]

Axworthy responded to the failed hit by condemning Mossad for using Canadian passports, which could have led to a Canadian being mistakenly killed in retaliation. He also recalled Canada's ambassador to Israel. But, within a week of these actions Axworthy accepted Israel's "expression of regret" (not a "direct apology") for disguising its agents as Canadians. Israel's Foreign Minister, David Levy, sent Axworthy the following message: "I wish to assure you that the concern of the government and people of Canada are fully appreciated and that steps have been taken by the relevant authorities in Israel to avoid a recurrence of similar incidents in the future."[24] This paved the way for a resumption of full diplomatic relations.

In response to the Liberal government's rebuke of Israeli actions Spector, who was appointed by a Conservative government, claimed CSIS and Mossad agents met days before the attempt to assassinate Meshal.[25] He said Ottawa wanted to cover up Israel's use of fake Canadian passports.[26] "Canadian authorities knew, in general, that passports were being used by Mossad," Spector noted. "It was known to people at the embassy and they essentially turned a blind eye to it."[27] According to Spector, CSIS supported Mossad missions in exchange for intelligence. "Israeli operational agents have been given to understand that the use of Canadian passports is the quid pro quo [for information on Arab immigrants]."[28]

Ottawa's response to the Meshal hit gives credence to Spector's claims. The book *Kill Khalid* explains: "Given the history of Israel's abuse of Canadian passports, Ottawa's retaliation was surprisingly light — the brief recall of Ambassador David Berger. There was no threat — or even a hint — of trade sanctions, nor of tougher visa conditions for Israelis wishing to enter Canada. And certainly there was no suggestion that there might be an application to extradite the Mossad hit men — 'A' and 'D' — to face charges in Canada. Ottawa, it seemed, just wanted the whole thing to go away."[29]

The Meshal incident, which prompted Ottawa to modify the Canadian passport, didn't affect the Mossad-CSIS relationship. A Canadian working for Mossad, Jonathan Ross, explained in his 2008 book: "The Canadian Security and Intelligence Service was sympathetic, and it was business as usual with them despite the diplomatic flap. During a liaison exchange by our [Mossad] counterterrorism officers to Canada soon after the affair broke, many CSIS members mentioned that their only regret in the whole affair was that we didn't succeed [in assassinating Meshal]."[30]

A few weeks after the Meshal incident blew over a Canadian living in Israel, Leslie Lewis, told Ottawa he was contacted by the Bureau of Immigration Affairs, a presumed Mossad front. A year earlier, Lewis gave the Israelis his expired passport and other identification. Uncomfortable with the Meshal hit, Lewis rejected the new request for his Canadian passport.[31] "The presumed Mossad front also pressed his daughter, Devora, to apply for a Canadian passport, and then to return to Israel, where she would hand the new travel document to the Israelis."[32] Ottawa launched an investigation into Lewis' accusations. But, reported the *Globe and Mail*: "Intelligence sources say investigation is incomplete because Ottawa did not want to upset Israel."[33] One intelligence official told the *Globe*: "They [Canadian officials] got the answers they wanted from the Israelis and ended it right there. Some investigation." Another source said: "It is a farce."[34]

In September 2002 Israel's secret services were once again accused of using Canadian cover. A Palestinian alleged that men pretending to be Canadians took him to the embassy in Tel Aviv and promised to help him emigrate to Canada if he spied for them.[35] Akram Zatmeh said he supplied the "Canadians" with information that helped Israel pinpoint the whereabouts of a senior Hamas official, Sheik Salah Shehadeh, who was killed 20 minutes later by a rocket from an Israeli F-16. Fired into a residential building in Gaza, the missile killed 14, including nine children.[36] If Zatmeh's story is true it is hard to believe that Israeli agents could, or would, take a Palestinian into the Tel Aviv Embassy without the knowledge of at least some Canadian officials.

Mossad has a history of approaching Canadians to do its dirty work. During the UN's mid-1980s mission along the Syria/Israel border Mossad recruited Canadian peacekeepers. *By Way of Deception* describes how Mossad agents targeted "particularly the Canadians ... [because] they felt in Israel as if they were in a Western country, so they were quite comfortable — a lot more so than in an Arab country. ... There were several Canadian duvshanim (literally honey pies, UN peacekeeping forces paid to transport messages and packages) transferring packages back and forth over the border for us [Mossad]."[37] The Israeli spy agency's favorite carrier was a Canadian UN officer stationed in Naharia, a coastal city in northern Israel close to the neutral zone separating it from Syria. "Free to cross the border at will," the officer was paid $500 to leave a hollowed-out rock with papers at a specified location on the road to Damascus.[38] It was then picked up by another Mossad agent.[39] The Canadian officer was part of a team that helped Israel track the Syrian military's preparedness.

In fact, the Harper government formalized some aspects of the Mossad/CSIS relationship. In early 2008 Ottawa signed a wide-ranging "border management and security" agreement with Israel, even though Canada doesn't share a border with that country.[40] The agreement is rather vague, but includes sharing information, cooperating on illegal immigration, cooperating on law enforcement etc.. The specifics were to be flushed out by a bilateral "Management Committee" established to identify priorities for the two governments and coordinate future security arrangements.[41]

Canadians for Justice and Peace in the Middle East make four main criticisms of the "border management and security" agreement:

"Question the fallacy of 'common threats.' Proponents of the assertion of 'common threats' used in the Declaration suggest that Canada and Israel face the same threats for the same reasons. This is not true. Israel faces hostility because of its military occupation of Palestinian territory — Canada only faces similar threats in as much as it endorses this occupation.

"Question the border security intents. Since Canada and Israel don't share a common border, it's perplexing as to why they would seek cooperation on border security. Canadians would want to demand that Canada have no role — direct or indirect — in the policing of Israel's shifting borders with Syria, Lebanon and the Palestinian Territories.

"Question the sharing of information with respect to immigration and ethnic profiling. Canadians should demand guarantees that Israeli intelligence — potentially obtained through torture — would not be used in Canadian immigration or refugee proceedings. Furthermore, Canadians must have guarantees that trumped up Israeli intelligence would not be used against Canadians domestically who are opposed to illicit Israeli practices. Canadians must also insist that Israel not have access to confidential files on Canadians.

"Question cooperation on prisons and correctional services ... Israeli prisons [where some 10 000 Palestinians languish] are a focal point of human rights abuses."[42]

The aftermath of 9/11 has led to a major rise in security-related visits to Israel by Canadian officials. Underlying these meetings is a George-Bush style "war on terror" mentality.

In the summer of 2005, 39 Ontario police chiefs and Ontario's Minister of Community Safety and Correctional Services went to "study Israel's anti-terrorism and law-enforcement strategies, and how it handles trauma."[43] The police chiefs were given "a demonstration of various Israeli High Tech security systems and products at an event in which 12 Israeli companies took part."[44] Half of the trip's bill was paid for by the Canadian Jewish Congress (Ontario) and United Jewish Appeal (Toronto).[45]

The First International Security Conference was held in Jerusalem in June 2008. The security conference brought together officials from the U.S., England, Germany, Italy, Poland, Spain, Canada and Israel to "promote and strengthen the co-operation between the countries and to share the knowledge, capabilities and experience accumulated among the countries during their war against terror while facing other homeland security challenges."[46]

Canada's ambassador in Tel Aviv, Jon Allen, told the Security Conference: "We live in a time when terrorists see the whole world as their field of action, and so must we. Because they enjoy global reach, we need unparalleled co-operation. Because they often operate at a sub-state level, we must adopt a transnational approach ourselves."[47]

The head of the Canadian military, Walter Natynczyk, echoed the ambassador's statement when he visited a number of

Israeli military installations in October 2009. He said the Canadian military has "really come to understand and appreciate what the Israeli forces have had to counter for quite some time and the techniques, the way and the procedures that the Israeli military has adopted and evolved over the past few decades."[48] Natynczyk continued: "I'm not sure if the Israeli standpoint is that much different than the Canadian standpoint, having had the experience in Afghanistan."[49]

Military

Natynczyk's tour, mentioned above, reflected the growing ties between the Canadian and Israeli military industrial complexes. Canada's military, arms companies and many private citizens aid the Israeli military in a variety of ways.

Despite its pattern of killing civilians, Ottawa invited the Israeli Air Force (IAF) to train in Canada. In spring 2005, 10 Israeli F16s and about 150 crew took part in NATO's (Israel is not a member) annual Maple Flag war games at Cold Lake Alberta.[50] "Israel arrived two weeks early and is staying a few extra weeks to take advantage of Cold Lake Air Weapons Range, one of the world's largest unrestricted air spaces," explained Lieutenant Sonia Connock, the public affairs officer for the Maple Flag exercise.[51] Alluding to the history of Cold Lake as a training ground for the British military, journalist Jon Elmer summarized the shift in orientation: "Good night Battle of Britain, good morning Gaza."[52]

Canada has supported the IAF in other ways, as well. In the late 1990s, Brampton-based Nortel won a $70 million contract to replace the IAF's communications infrastructure.[53] Through their ties to U.S. military contractors, a dozen Canadian firms made parts for infrared guidance systems, radar equipment and training simulators for Israel's F-15 Eagle tactical bomber, F-16 Fighting Falcon bomber and AH-64 Apache attack helicopter.[54] "Canadian companies and taxpayers played an important role in the production of much of the military equipment that is currently being used to bomb villages, neighbourhoods and key infrastructure in Lebanon," reported dominionpaper.ca during the 2006 war.[55] Additionally, between 2006 and 2008 the Canada Pension Plan (CPP) invested about $100 million in Boeing and Lockheed Martin, which produce the F-15, F-16 and Apache.[56]

To "advance industrial partnerships between Canadian and Israeli companies" the Canadian Association of Defence and Security Industries (CADSI), which has received hundreds of thousands of dollars in federal grants, organized a "Canada/Israel Industry Partnering Mission" in 2004.[57] Canada's Minister of National Defence, Israel's Ambassador to Canada, an official from Israel's Ministry of Defence and a number of top Canadian bureaucrats attended the gathering. Leading Israeli weapons makers such as Rafael, Simigon, Soltamheld Elbit, Elisra, Israeli Aircraft Industries and Israeli Military Industries made presentations at the conference and held "Company One-on-Ones" with their Canadian counterparts.[58]

The aim of the event was to strengthen ties between Canadian and Israeli arms producers. It appears to have borne fruit. Richmond B.C.-based MacDonald Dettwiler produced an unmanned drone with Israel Aerospace Industries while Bombardier worked on a maritime patrol aircraft with the same company. Toronto-based A.U.G. Signals and Israel's InfoWrap Systems "have established a partnership to develop intelligent video software for an integrated surveillance system, called the Detection and Identification for Video Surveillance Systems. The proposed system will be the first to enable reliable, automatic outdoor moving object identification, even during the night."[59] This technology would likely serve IDF operations in the occupied territories and the Canadian Forces who knows where.

Despite the IDF's many human rights violations, Canadian companies continue to sell weapons directly to Israel. According to an early 2009 Coalition to Oppose the Arms Trade (COAT) report, more than 140 Canadian weapons makers export products to Israel.[60] Canadian weapons sales to Israel included ammunition for small arms and some large caliber arms. "Canadian companies like Nortel and Bombardier, and smaller military companies like Frontline Robotics and MDA, are all working directly with the Israeli military. ... Mawashi Corp. in Quebec helps develop body armor used by the Israeli Border Police and Army in suppressing Palestinian demonstrations."[61]

To install security and surveillance equipment along the separation barrier/apartheid wall Israel's Defence Ministry contracted Senstar Magal Security Systems and Elbit Systems (a subsidiary of Koor, established by Montrealer Charles Bronfman). Senstar's massive office and manufacturing facility and 10-acre outdoor sensor test site in Carp, near Ottawa, helped develop a broad range of surveillance and intrusion detection related security products. The company completed 125 km of security refurbishments along the wall.[62]

Ties between Israeli and Canadian military companies are often underwritten with public funds. The Canada-Israel Industrial Research and Development Fund has pumped tens of millions of dollars into joint research ventures between the countries' technology companies, including many military specific projects.[63]

Canadian-owned Athlone Global Security (AGS) provides a good example of the ties between the Israeli military industrial complex and its North American counterpart. According to its website: "AGS Group capitalizes on Israel's robust HLS [homeland security] sector by systematically analyzing the most promising new technologies and selecting potential investments based on strict criteria of technological soundness, market potential, and management quality."[64]

AGS's board of directors have included many former high-ranking officials in the Canadian, Israeli and U.S. military and security establishments. Maj. Gen. (retired) Lewis W. MacKenzie, who served for 36 years in the Canadian military; Maj. Gen. (retired) Doron Almog, the former chief of the IDF's Southern Command; Lt. Gen. (retired) Jay Garner, who headed the post-war reconstruction of Iraq in 2003, are among the three countries' military and intelligence elite who have been on the company's board.[65]

There are numerous other ways in which Canada supports the Israeli army. "Un Montréalais part combattre en Israël," read *La Presse* during Israel's 2006 assault on Lebanon.[66] A few weeks later the *Canadian Jewish News* reported, "Canadian youths leave home to join Israeli army."[67]

There is no figure available on Canadians in the IDF, but at least 25 volunteers from the Greater Toronto Area fought in Gaza during Israel's 22-day 2008/2009 assault.[68]

While it is technically illegal for Canadians to recruit for a foreign army a number of organizations in Canada promote the IDF. A regular advertisement in the *Canadian Jewish News* for sar-el.org may contravene the Foreign Enlistment Act. "Express your Zionism by serving as a civilian volunteer on an Israeli army supply base," proclaimed a November 2009 ad.

Numerous charities, many with the ability to provide tax receipts, (see following chapter for more on charities) support the IDF in one way or another. Just a few examples follow:

"Effort under way to launch fund to support IDF soldiers," noted the *Canadian Jewish News* in July 2009.[69] One example is Aid to Disabled Veterans of Israel or Beit Halochem (Canada), which brings soldiers singled out as heroes by the IDF on trips to Canada. Many Canadians, including the Charles R. Bronfman foundation, support the Libi Fund — "The Fund For Strengthening Israel's Defense."[70]

In early 2008 Major Gil Chemke, a member of the IDF's elite search and rescue team, toured the country on behalf of the Canadian Magen David Adom for Israel (CMDAI). Established to assist wounded soldiers and the population during disasters, in 2002 CMDAI won a legal battle over Revenue Canada after it revoked the organization's charitable status for operating in the occupied territories. Chemke drummed up financial contributions for CMDAI by showing "behind-the-scenes video footage of a rescue operation in Lebanon for a female air crew member whose helicopter was shot down by Hezbollah" during Israel's 2006 assault on Lebanon.[71]

Established in 1971 the Association for the Soldiers of Israel in Canada (ASI) provides financial and moral support to active duty soldiers. A June 2009 *Canadian Jewish News* advertisement explained "the Association for the soldiers of Israel invites you to show your support for the brave youth of the IDF at our gala dinner."[72] In 2009 ASI (Canada), which provides tax-receipts through the Canadian Zionist Cultural Association, and El Al airlines granted a 50% discount on flights to Israel from Canada for families of "lone soldiers."[73]

Prominent Toronto couple Heather Reisman and Gerry Schwartz, who own or control more than two thirds of Chapters/Indigo/Coles bookstores, created the "Heseg Foundation for Lone Soldiers". Reisman and Schwartz provide up to $3 million per year for post-military scholarships to individuals without family in Israel who join the IDF.[74] After completing their military service these non-Israeli "lone soldiers" gain access to this scholarship money. For the IDF high command — the Heseg Board includes a number of generals and a former head of Mossad — "lone soldiers" are of value beyond their military capacities. Foreigners volunteering to fight for Israel are a powerful symbol to pressure Israelis weary of IDF behaviour. Schwartz and Reisman's support for Heseg has spurred a campaign to boycott Chapters/Indigo/Coles, which controls 70% of Canada's retail book trade.

Of course ties between Canadian non-governmental institutions and Israel's military go back decades. Just after Israel invaded Egypt in 1956, for instance, B'nai Brith Eastern Canada adopted a Soldiers Club in Eilat, the country's southernmost city.[75] In a particularly disturbing comment on Israel's supporters, aggression has been good for fundraising. $9.2 million was raised in 1948-49.[76] After the June 1967 war, leading Canadian capitalist Samuel Bronfman initiated a $25 million campaign for Israel.[77] Similarly, during the October 1973 war Canadians sent $54 million to Israel and bought $50 million in Israel Bonds.[78] More recently, after Israel's summer 2006 destruction of Lebanon another $42 million was raised.[79]

Business

Beyond intelligence and military links some ties between Canada and the illegal occupation of Palestinian lands have been more direct. Companies involved in the Trans-Israel Highway, for example, developed the infrastructure of occupation. Toronto-based engineering company AECON operates the Trans-Israel Highway's tolls.[80]

The Canadian Highways Infrastructure Corporation led a private sector consortium that built this multibillion-dollar highway, the largest infrastructure project in Israeli history.[81] "By bringing Israeli cities, towns and settlements on both sides of the Green Line together into one grid, the Trans-Israel Highway moves the country's population center eastward, reconfiguring the entire country."[82] Running along the 1967 border, the Trans-Israel Highway is designed to be "the new central spine of the country," linking Israel proper to the West Bank bypass roads.[83] Access to these bypass highways is restricted to persons with specially designated license plates to distinguish Jews from non-Jews.[84] Zmag.org editor Justin Podur explains: "Israel's network of bypass roads is designed very deliberately to reach from the core areas of Israel itself into settlements in the West Bank without allowing traffic or communication between West Bank towns. These bypass roads are an integral component of ... the 'matrix of control', by which Palestinians are isolated, surrounded, and disconnected from each other, made wholly dependent on the whims of the Israeli regime. It is an appalling program of imprisoning an entire population. It is also good business for the Canadian Highways Infrastructure Corporation."[85]

A number of other Canadian corporations also aid Israel's occupation. In July 2008 a West Bank village filed suit in Montreal Superior Court against two Quebec-based companies, Green Park International and Green Mount International, for building an Israeli settlement in the West Bank. The town of Bil'in claimed the Canadian companies built part of Israel's largest settlement, Modiin Illit, on land seized after Israel captured the West Bank. "The defendants ... as de facto agents of the State of Israel are, and have been, illegally constructing residential and other buildings," the suit reads.[86] "In so doing, the defendants are aiding, abetting, assisting and conspiring with the state of Israel in carrying out an illegal purpose."[87]

While two Canadian companies were accused of abetting an "illegal purpose" another helped build West Bank law enforcement. During 2006-2007 Brampton-based Nortel operated a 'Smart City' pilot project in the West Bank settlement of Ariel. "For the project, Nortel set-up a WLAN [wireless local area network] 'mesh network' allowing the settlement to control wireless surveillance cameras, remotely monitor water meters, and to carryout 'wireless municipal law enforcement functions.' Nortel considered the Ariel contract 'a showpiece project' that helped the company emphasize the relevance and reliability of its WLAN 'mesh-networks' for both civilian and military applications."[88]

Canadian companies operating in the Occupied Territories have taken their cue from Ottawa. In an implicit recognition of the occupation, Canada's 1997 free trade agreement with Israel includes the West Bank as a place where the country's custom laws are applied. Canada's trade agreement is based on the areas Israel maintains territorial control over, not on internationally recognized borders. The European Union's trade agreement with Israel, on the other hand, explicitly excludes products from territory Israel captured in the 1967 war and occupies against international law.[89]

Ontario, Alberta, Manitoba and Quebec all followed the federal government and signed trade agreements with Israel. In September 2008 Raymond Bachand, Quebec's Economic Development Minister, explained that "by signing this complementary agreement, Quebec is reiterating the attachment it has with Israel and its wish for a closer collaboration in the future."[90] It is not clear if Quebec City is "attached" to Israel's occupation of the West Bank since the Quebec-Israel economic agreement provides no way to ensure that Israel respects international law regarding settlement construction or Palestinian human rights.

Chapter 6
Charity begins at home

Charitable activity is an under-explored aspect of Canadian foreign policy. Who receives financial support largely reflects a society's political culture and the Israel-Palestine conflict suggests there is significant room to favour one side or the other. Charities are authorized under the Canadian Charities Act of 1967, giving Ottawa a powerful tool to make it easy or hard for organizations to raise money. Groups with official charitable status can provide tax credits for donations, meaning that up to 25% of their budgets effectively come from public coffers. Organizations unable to provide tax receipts are at a disadvantage.

The government has other tools to favour one side or another, as well. Many Palestinian groups cannot raise money in Canada because it's illegal for Canadians to support numerous organizations involved in the conflict. Ottawa's post-9/11 terrorist list makes it illegal to send money to the democratic Hamas government and a half dozen other Palestinian organizations.[1] Only one Israeli group, the marginal Kahane Chai, is on the list.[2] It is legal, for instance, to provide financial support to charities that support a foreign army, the IDF, but not Hezbollah. It's also legal to send money to institutions occupying the West Bank and even — although it's a grey area — in many cases to claim a tax credit for these donations.

Canadian charitable activity in Israel/Palestine and Ottawa's policy towards those activities further demonstrates a bias towards one side in the conflict.

***

A mid-1990s survey found that there were more than 300 registered Canadian charities with ties to Israel.[3] In 1991 the *Ottawa Citizen* estimated that Canadian Jews sent more than $100 million a year to Israel and possibly as much as $200 million (with inflation this number would have more than doubled by 2010).[4]

At least some of this money made its way to build and support settlements Ottawa officialy deems illegal under international law.

A 1996 *Toronto Star* investigation revealed that a number of Canadian organizations used their charitable status to issue tax receipts for contributions to the settlements.[5] Tax lawyer David Drache claimed "there are hundreds of [Canadian] organizations ... supporting organizations directly or indirectly beyond the Green Line [the international border that demarcates Israel from the West Bank]."[6]

It's not clear how much Canadian money makes its way to the settlements. But the amount is significant. In the late 1990s Israel's largest settler group, Yesha, raised more than $700,000 a year in Canada.[7] When Ariel Sharon visited Canada in the mid-1990s, according to the Canadian Arab Federation's Jehad Al-Iweiwi, he "left with more than $1 million in tax-deductible funds, with no secret as to the destination."[8]

According to one legal interpretation, Canadians shouldn't be able to claim a tax rebate for money sent to Israeli institutions enabling the occupation. Tax law in this area should be determined by Canadian foreign policy, which (officially) considers the West Bank illegally occupied. In the late 1990s judge Neil Barclay ruled: "To allow Canadian charities to assist in providing the religious institutions and the health, education and other social services that encourage and sustain Israeli settlement in the Occupied Territories would be fundamentally at odds with Canada's position" on the matter.[9]

In 1996 the Toronto Zionist Council's charitable status was revoked for supporting settlements.[10] Revenue Canada did the same thing to the Toronto-based Press Foundation in late 1999. The *Toronto Star* revealed that Canadian callers to the New York-based Hebron Fund, which raised funds for settlers in Hebron, were given step-by-step instructions on sending donations through Press Foundation in exchange for a tax-deductible receipt.[11] "Toronto

Jews are one of our biggest supporters, they're tremendous," explained Judy Grossman from the Hebron Fund.[12]

Press Foundation also fundraised for settlements in the Golan Heights, which was taken from Syria during the 1967 war. The Golan Residents Committee urged supporters to "contribute whatever you can by sending your tax-deductible contribution to our offices abroad."[13] Canadian donors were instructed to direct donations through Press Foundation.[14] Even though Revenue Canada initially became concerned about the Press Foundation's activities in 1991, they only acted after its support for the settlements became totally blatant. Additionally, Revenue Canada did not retroactively challenge receipts issued improperly by Press Foundation, which raised as much as $5 million annually.[15]

Throughout the 1990s Revenue Canada only pursued the most flagrant breaches of the law. To be fair, it's a difficult job. Nearly 10% of Israel's Jewish population lives on territory occupied since 1967 so there isn't always a clear line between Israel and the settlements. Are donations to Hebrew University for bursaries given to settlers tax-deductible? How about funding for the Livnot program where Canadian Jews spend some time with settlers? What about money funneled to an Israeli charity working with another group active in the occupied territories?

Throughout the 1990s Revenue Canada (now Canada Revenue Agency) did not challenge any of these examples even if they could or should have. But at the end of the decade Revenue Canada's interpretation of Canadian policy was challenged. Reversing an earlier decision, in September 2002 the "Court of Appeal held that the position taken by the CRA with regard to the Green Line was wrong and that as a matter of law there was no reason why charitable work could not be carried on both in Israel proper and beyond the 1967 border. In effect, the court ruled that the approach used by the CRA for at least the past 10 years was an incorrect interpretation of what is meant by 'public policy.'"[16]

At print time there had been no further development on the legality of charities directing money to Israeli settlers.[17] If this judgment is allowed to stand organizations will be able to openly fundraise for illegal settlements and have Canadian taxpayers subsidize it. While this situation should make many Canadians angry, this country has a long history of using "charity" to support activities in Israel that go against the principles of Canada's Charter of Rights and Freedoms.

***

To create a predominantly Jewish country Zionist forces depopulated 450 Palestinian villages in 1947/48.[18] Then Israel tried to erase any trace of the former Arab inhabitants. Many Canadians supported Israel's move to colonize this recently conquered territory. In June 1961, "The Jewish National Fund report[ed] a 500,000 tree Canada Forest in the Judean Hills, six other Canadian sponsored woods tracts developed by Canadian donors and 75 km of 'boulevards' lining Negev and other roads."[19] The next year Israel established a Canadian village.[20] Subsequently, JNF Canada paid for the creation of the Toronto Community Forest in the Judean Hills, as well as a 25,000-tree New Brunswick Forest and Ottawa Recreation and Picnic Area in the Negev.[21]

The Jewish National Fund (JNF) Canada raised $15 million ($80m in 2009 money) to build Canada Park on territory captured during the 1967 war.[22] A 3,200 acre recreational area, the park overlooks the fertile Ayalon Valley between Jerusalem and Tel Aviv. From 1973 to 1995 Canadian benefactors planted more than five million trees on the land.[23] A JNF brochure described the park as a "tribute to Canada and to the Canadian Jewish community whose vision and foresight helped transform a barren stretch of land into a major recreational area."[24] Notwithstanding JNF claims, the park contributed to the displacement of 5,000 people.[25] Three peaceful villages were demolished to make way for Canada Park.[26] An IDF reservist, Amos Kenan, described the destruction: "The unit commander told us that it had been decided to blow up three villages in our sector; they were Beit Nuba, Imwas and Yalu. There were old people who could hardly walk, murmuring old women, mothers carrying babies, small children. The children wept and asked for water. They all carried white flags ... we were told to block the entrances of the villages and prevent inhabitants [from] returning ... the order was issued [to fire] over their heads and tell them not to enter the village."[27]

Despite repeatedly attempting to return home, the expelled Palestinians were not allowed back. A 1986 UN Special Committee reported to the Secretary-General: "[we] consider it a matter of deep concern that these villagers have persistently been denied the right to return to their land on which Canada Park has been built by the JNF Canada and where the Israeli authorities are reportedly planning to plant a forest instead of allowing the reconstruction of the destroyed villages."[28] The JNF Canada, which launched a $7 million campaign to refurbish the park in 2007, replaced most traces of Palestinian history with signs about Canada.[29] "Walking around the park [in 2007] the only visible signs of previous inhabitants are a crumbling cemetery with stones engraved in Arabic and a series of old village walls. Some of these near the park entrance bear rows of plaques to Canadian donors — the city of Ottawa, the Metropolitan Toronto Police Department, former Ontario premier Bill Davis and Toronto city councillor Joe Pantalone."[30] Inaugurated by former Prime Minister John Diefenbaker in 1975, the Diefenbaker Parkway bisects the park.[31]

After learning about the situation in 1978, Palestinian Canadian Ismail Zayid tried to get Ottawa to investigate the use of charitable donations to build Canada Park.[32] Three decades later prominent Palestinian human rights organization, Al-Haq, released a report blaming the Israeli government, JNF Canada and the federal government for the violation of international law and human rights caused by Canada Park. Al-Haq argued that Ottawa was partly responsible for the Palestinians' dispossession since the federal government provided tax rebates for donations to the JNF.[33]

In 2007 Lebanese-Canadian Ronald Saba filed a detailed complaint concerning the JNF's charitable status with the Canadian Human Rights Commission. Saba's complaint dealt with Canada Park and JNF policy more generally. The claim was leveled at the "Government of Canada for violating the Canadian Human Rights Act and Canada Revenue Agency Policy Statement CPS-021 by subsidizing racial discrimination through granting and maintaining charitable status for the Jewish National Fund."[34] Canadian officials refused to seriously investigate this complaint or follow-up ones.

Established in 1910 JNF Canada is one of the more important Israel-focused charities registered in Canada. It raises about $10 million annually in tax-deductible donations. Despite projecting itself "as an environmentally friendly organization concerned with ecology and sustainable development," it is a linchpin of Zionist colonialism.[35]

In the early 1900s the JNF bought land from absentee property owners and drove out the Palestinians tilling it. Much of the JNF's land, on which 70% of Israel's population lives, was stolen from Palestinians during the 1947/48 war.[36] For years it built roads to facilitate IDF operations, including in the occupied territories.[37] A 1971 JNF brochure explained: "At the request of the Defense Forces the JNF has since 1967 completed a 150-km road along the Jordan River border, primarily for the use of military patrols; a network of roads to army positions in the Golan Heights and lower Jordan Valley; a road connecting the Etsyon Bloc to the Jerusalem Hill settlements, and two roads up Mount Hermon."[38]

For fundraising purposes the JNF presents itself as a charitable institution. Yet, it regularly organizes political speaking events designed partly to influence Canadian foreign policy. In February 1990 Israeli Foreign Minister Moshe Arens told a 750 strong JNF Toronto audience that Israel will "never" negotiate with the Palestine

Liberation Organization.[39] More recently, the JNF lobbied for war. In 2007 it sponsored a cross-Canada speaking tour by Col. Ze'ev Raz who led Israel's 1981 bombing of Iraq's nuclear reactor. The aim of the tour was to build momentum for an attack against Iran. "Sanctions against Iran are not effective," Raz explained. "Sanctions are too vulnerable to cheating. The only solution to the Iran problem is for there to be an effort of the U.S. and other forces to invade Iran from the ground." Col. Raz continued, "If the U.S. doesn't do it, then Israel will have to send fighters into Iran, but that won't solve the problem. There have to be ground forces sent into Iran."[40]

In mid-2009 JNF Canada announced an "Ambassadors" program to send 15 to 20 volunteers to Israel annually. They will be trained "to become representatives for JNF and Israel, to communicate the virtues of the Holy Land to organizations that don't normally hear about the JNF in Canada, such as church groups."[41] At the end of 2009 the JNF organized a talk by Hillel Neuer, executive director of UN Watch, titled "The Goldstone Report: Tainted to the Core."

With quasi state status in Israel the JNF is a racist institution that discriminates in favour of Jews.[42] Shutting out Israeli Arabs, JNF lands can only be leased by Jews. In May 2002 JNF Canada's executive-director for Eastern Canada, Mark Mendelson, explained: "We are trustees between world Jewry and the land of Israel."[43] JNF Canada's head Frank A. Wilson echoed this statement in July 2009: "JNF are the caretakers of the Land of Israel on behalf of its owners, who are the Jewish people everywhere around the world."[44]

In June 1981 the *Globe and Mail* reported on a JNF-Canada financed Israeli government campaign to "Judaize" the Galilee, a largely Arab northern region of Israel. "The Government is building Jewish settlements on our land, surrounding us and turning our villages into ghettos," said Khateeb Raja, mayor of Deir Hanna, an Arab town in the Galilee. Ishi Mimon told the *Globe* he planned to move his family to the newly settled "Galil Canada" area because "the Galilee should have a Jewish majority." JNF Canada's representative in Israel, Akiva Einis, described the political objective of Galil Canada: "The Government decided to stop the wholesale plunder (by Israeli Arabs) of state lands [conquered in 1947/48]. ... The settlements are all on mountain tops and look out over large areas of land. If an Arab squatter takes a plow onto land that is not his, the settlers lodge a complaint with the police."[45]

JNF Canada spent tens of millions of dollars ($35 million was the total fundraising target) on 14 Jewish settlements in Galil Canada.[46] In the contested valley of Lotem a stone wall and monument was erected with "hundreds of small plaques etched with names and home towns of Canadians who have contributed money to the Galilee settlements." Most of the donors to Galil Canada were Jewish, "but a Pentecostal congregation in Vancouver, the Glad Tidings Temple, has given $1-million."[47] Tawfiz Daggash, Deir Hanna's deputy mayor, denounced Canadian financial support for the settlements. "I want to say to the people of Canada that every dollar they contribute [to JNF] is helping the Israeli Government in its attempt to destroy the Arab people here."[48]

A 1998 UN Committee on Economic, Social and Cultural Rights found that the JNF systematically discriminated against Arab Israelis.[49] According to the UN report, JNF lands are "chartered to benefit Jews exclusively," which has led to an "institutionalized form of discrimination."[50] In 2005 Israel's Supreme Court came to similar conclusions. It found that the JNF, which owns 13% of the country's land and has significant influence over most of the rest, systematically excluded Arab Israelis from leasing its property.[51]

Despite its racist practices a number of provincial governments have agreements with the JNF. Manitoba and JNF-Canada, Prairie region, signed a partnership in 2006 to promote technology and research intended to assist communities in both northern Manitoba and Israel.[52] "The three-year, $1-million environmental research partnership will focus on improving the environment in both regions through forest diversification, water innovation and rapid-growth greenhouse technology."[53] The JNF signed a similar deal with Alberta's Ministry of Infrastructure in 2005. Both sides contributed $1 million to research the design, construction and rehabilitation of water management and irrigation infrastructure for drought-stricken areas.[54]

The JNF's ties to public institutions and officials go beyond its partnerships with provincial governments or its charity status. Liberal Senator Yoine Goldstein is an Executive Officer of JNF Canada and the organization has long been supported by a who's who of the Canadian political elite. Former prime ministers John Diefenbaker, Lester Pearson and Brian Mulroney have spoken at JNF events.[55] In 2001 the JNF Toronto's 53rd annual dinner included former Ontario premier Bill Davis, provincial Liberal Leader Dalton McGuinty, Attorney-General David Young and then Mayor Mel Lastman.[56]

***

After 1948 Israel needed immigrants to "Judaize" its newly acquired landscape. A number of charitable organizations in addition to JNF Canada supported Canadian emigration to Israel, which reached 1,500 by 1961.[57] Part of the Jewish Agency for Israel, Montreal's Aliyah Center promoted immigration from just after Israel's founding until 2009. Toronto still has an Israeli immigration centre but most Canadian cities' Israel immigration services have been moved online.[58]

Because we are a rich and relatively tolerant country only a small fraction of Canada's Jewish community emigrated to Israel. Canadians have, however, financed a great deal of emigration from poorer parts of the world. In the years after Israel's creation a significant proportion of the money raised by Canadian Zionists facilitated this immigration. In 1951 Canadians put up $5.25 million for Israel to absorb 600,000 Jews over three years while the 1960 United Jewish Appeal (Toronto) fundraising drive was largely promoted as a way to raise money for Israel to absorb 345,000 poorly integrated immigrants.[59]

For many years State of Israel Bonds helped support Jewish immigration. First sold in 1951, promoting bond sales was a priority for pro-Israel activists. With the new state having difficulty raising money on Wall Street, bonds were "securities issued by the State of Israel to help build the nation's infrastructure."[60] Thirty-five years after the first bond was sold they still represented 10% of Israel's foreign capital requirements.[61] Canadians were the highest per-capita investors in Israel Bonds.[62] During the first four decades of bond sales Canada accounted for more than $1 billion of $13 billion sold worldwide.[63] Steadily increasing over the years, in 1999 Canadian sales topped $100 million.[64]

Advertised on Montreal's leading English language radio stations, Israel Bonds have received widespread support. In the late 1980s more than a third of all bond sales were made to non-Jews.[65] Canada's major banks all bought bonds and participated in bond-financing plans.[66] In 1980 Michel Belanger, president of the Banque National du Canada, explained why they acquired bonds. "[Purchasing Israel Bonds] is an occasion for investors to show their interest in the economic development of Israel first and foremost but also the economic relations between Israel, Canada and Quebec ... [Buying Israel bonds] is above all else a gesture of friendship, a gesture of confidence in the development possibilities of Israel and its eventual economic relations with Canada and Quebec."[67]

The bonds have received high-level political support. In 1990 Governor General Jeanne Sauve was an official bonds promoter.[68] Prime Minister Brian Mulroney told a 1988 Israel bond dinner: "I am the heir of the rich spiritual and cultural legacy of Israel, which is the core of Western civilization. I have admired modern Israel in the way one admires a miracle."[69] Twenty-seven years earlier Prime Minister John Diefenbaker spoke at a bonds dinner.[70] Diefenbaker, reported the *Canadian Jewish News*, "declared that we welcome the assistance and support which Jewish Canadians are giving Israel."[71]

In 1960 Samuel Bronfman and a number of other leading Jewish capitalists took Ottawa's advice and established the Canada-Israel Development Corporation. With an initial $5 million outlay its goal was to "attract investment from the Canadian public... for industry in Israel basic to Israel's economy."[72]

Since the state's creation Canadians have also provided important financial support to Israel's universities. In June 1961 the *Canadian Jewish News* reported: "The names of buildings at the Hebrew University, the Weizmann Institute, the Technion and Bar Ilan University, all sound like rosters of Canadian Jewry."[73]

In recent decades Canadian capitalists, subsidized through tax receipts, have put tens of millions of dollars into Israeli universities. Barrick Gold Chairman Peter Munk, who "suggested that Israel's survival is dependent on maintaining its technological superiority over the Arabs," raised $18.5-million for Technion (Israel Institute of Technology).[74] In 2006 Technion opened the Peter Munk Research Institute. That same year Munk's mining associate, Seymour Schulich, gave $20 million (US) to Technion's faculty of chemistry, which now bears his name.[75]

There is a Canadian Technion Society as well as a Canadian Friends of Haifa University, Tel Aviv University, Hebrew University, etc. Begun in 1956, Canadian Friends of Hebrew University now has chapters across the country.[76] Facilitated by its charitable status, in 2009 it planned to raise $50 million over eight years for Hebrew University's Institute for Medical Research Israel-Canada.[77]

As a show of gratitude to Canadian Friends of Hebrew University, the school named a prominent dormitory Canada House in the mid-1990s.[78] The Hebrew University dedicated other buildings to this country's citizenry. To thank the Bronfman family for its largesse, Hebrew University established the Seagram Center in 1981 while it opened an Asper centre for Entrepreneurship after Izzy Asper donated $5 million in the late 1990s.[79]

Chapter 7
Political Parties

Liberal and Conservative support

Support for Israel usually crosses party lines, as two examples during the Trudeau government demonstrate. During a debate a week after the UN voted to accept PLO participation in 1974, Conservative and Liberal MPs agreed that Israel needed to okay the PLO's participation at a UN conference.[1] The next year the UN passed a resolution equating Zionism with racism. A day after the Zionism-equals-racism vote the House of Commons unanimously condemned it.[2]

Both Liberal and Conservative governments — from Louis Saint Laurent to John Diefenbaker, Brian Mulroney to Paul Martin — proclaimed their love of Israel. Just after Israel's founding External Affairs Minister (and later prime minister) Louis Saint Laurent noted: "I am happy that my government can make a contribution to the creation of a Jewish state in Palestine. This is the realization of a divine prophecy in our time."[3] In 1961 Diefenbaker, who received a humanitarian award from Israel's Histradut labour federation, explained that "in rebuilding the land of their forefathers the people of Israel also bear witness to those moral and religious truths that find supreme and imperishable expression in the Bible."[4] Eight years later Lester Pearson's External Affairs Minister, Paul Martin Sr., called Israel "the greatest achievement of nationhood of all time."[5]

The first intifada (uprising) broke out in 1987. Eerily similar to Prime Minister Harper's comment on Lebanon two decades later, Brian Mulroney told the CBC that Israel's brutal suppression of rock-throwing Palestinian youth was handling the situation with "restraint."[6] When questioned by a CBC reporter about the similarity between the plight of Palestinians and Blacks in South Africa, Mulroney replied that any comparison between Israel and South

Africa was "false and odious and should never be mentioned in the same breath."[7] In 1993, six years into Israel's brutal suppression of the Palestinian uprising Mulroney boldly proclaimed his support for that country. "Israel is more than just a country, it is the embodiment of the spiritual values that have shaped Western civilization."[8] At the September 1987 Francophonie summit in Quebec City, Canada was the only country (41 participated) that failed to support a resolution calling for Palestinian self-determination. External Affairs Minister Joe Clark explained: "self-determination is a phrase we've had a lot of difficulty with. We think it could be a synonym for the establishment of an independent Palestinian state. The use of that language could prejudice the results of a conference on the Palestinians."[9] Eighteen months later Joe Clark reminded everyone of Ottawa's position: "I want to take this occasion to reiterate that Canada does not recognize the Palestinian state proclaimed last November."[10]

More than a decade after most of the world supported the PLO's admission to the UN, in December 1988 U.S. President Ronald Reagan finally agreed to initiate low-level contacts with the PLO. Ottawa refused to follow Washington's lead. "External Affairs Minister Joe Clark says Canada will not upgrade its relations with the PLO even though the United States is doing so."[11] Abdullah Abdullah, the PLO's representative in Ottawa, complained that "Canada is now the last country in the world outside of Israel that does not formally deal with the PLO."[12]

Jean Chretien, who became prime minister at the start of the Oslo peace negotiations, was the least 'Israel no matter what' Canadian prime minister since Pierre Trudeau. Still, Chretien's Ottawa definitely backed Israel and the "peace process" provided a good opportunity to expand economic ties.

In the early 1990s the federal government launched the Canada Israel Industrial Research and Development Foundation (CIIRDF). The multi-million dollar fund was created to match up hi-tech companies in the two countries. An August 1994 Memorandum of Understanding committed the two governments to: "(a) Promote the activities of their respective private sectors to increase the level of bilateral industrial research and development joint venture cooperation; (b) Facilitate the identification of specific projects or partnerships between Israeli and Canadian companies that could lead to industrial R&D cooperation; (c) Coordinate and focus suitable government resources and programmes to support closer commercial relations and industrial cooperation, including the establishment of a joint industrial R&D cooperation Initiative; (d) Give expression to this initiative through the establishment of a Canada Israel Industrial R&D programme (CIIRD) that will identify private sector interests, execute a complementarity study of Canadian and Israeli industrial R&D capabilities in priority sectors, and identify specific Canada/Israel matches for possible joint venture cooperation."[13] Renewed until 2010 the $20 million agreement makes Israel "Canada's longest-standing technology partner."[14] A positive Foreign Affairs assessment explained: "Our analysis revealed that most firms would not have conducted the R&D project without CIIRDF funding ... Our analysis based on sales forecasts from eleven Canadian firms undertaking CIIRDF R&D projects since 1999, estimated that $714.5 million in cumulative sales revenues and $178.6 million in cumulative profits will likely be generated by 2013."[15]

Chretien also signed a free trade accord with Israel. In January 1997 Israel became Canada's fourth free trade partner and first outside the Western hemisphere (after the U.S., Mexico and Chile). The agreement expanded upon an August 1993 Memorandum of Understanding on Economic Cooperation and a Joint Economic Commission begun in 1976.[16]

"Canada-Israel trade soars in wake of pact," noted a 1997 issue of *Canadian Jewish News*.[17] Bilateral trade between Canada and Israel topped a billion dollars and since signing the accord

"Canada has consistently suffered from a trade deficit with Israel."[18] In 2007 Canadian exports to Israel totaled $426.6 million while imports were $959.3 million.[19] Direct investment between the countries is three to four billion dollars.[20]

More than other Canadian governments, Chretien's was willing to censure Israel at the UN. Still, it often chose to be isolated in defending Israeli actions. In January 1997, the UN overwhelmingly passed a resolution calling for Israel to stop its massive bombardment of Lebanon and to withdraw its forces from Lebanese territory. The U.S. and Israel were the only countries to oppose the resolution. Canada abstained.[21]

To celebrate Israel's 50th birthday, in 1998 the Canadian International Development Agency (CIDA) and its Israeli counterpart, Mashav, financed a project in post-war Guatemala. Benjamin Abileah, a senior advisor at Mashav, said: "He [Foreign Affairs Minister Lloyd Axworthy] suggested that for Israel's 50th anniversary, Canada and Israel would mark it by doing a joint project of assistance in a developing country."[22]

A few months after celebrating 50 years of Israeli statehood Axworthy tried to dissuade Yasir Arafat from unilaterally declaring a Palestinian state in the West Bank and Gaza as per the initial Oslo Accords. "We don't think (it's) appropriate," Axworthy said in March 1999. "We still believe a negotiated settlement is the most effective way of getting a peace settlement."[23] Axworthy claimed to support a Palestinian state but only if arrived at through negotiations.[24] Four months later Ottawa heeded Washington's call to block a UN "conference on measures to implement the Fourth Geneva Convention in the Occupied Palestinian Territories, including Jerusalem."[25] Foreign Affairs pushed to postpone the mid-1999 conference, saying the issue had become "politicized," and could harm the "peace process."[26]

Rejected by its Arab neighbours, for years Israel was the only country not represented in a UN regional grouping. In the late

1990s Ottawa was "instrumental in formulating a consensus among European countries in favor of Israel's admission to the WEOG [Western Europe and Others Group]."[27]

Since 1967 Israel has controlled the lives of Palestinians without allowing them to vote in the country's elections. This did not stop Chretien from declaring: "Israel stands alone as a beacon of popular democracy in the Middle East."[28] A few months later, in April 2000, Chretien added: "The security of Israel is foremost among the concerns of Canada."[29]

Failing to see the benefits of the "peace negotiations," in October 2000 Palestinians rose up in a second Intifada. Once again Canada was isolated in its support for Israel. Against world opinion, in December 2000 Ottawa opposed a proposal to send 2,000 unarmed military observers to the Occupied Territories. Canada, alongside the U.S., France, Britain and the Netherlands, refused to support the UN resolution.[30] Ottawa said it could not vote for a force without Israel's, the occupying power, consent.[31]

In April 2002 Israel killed more than 50 Palestinians (initial reports were much higher) in Jenin. In response the UN Commission on Human Rights (UNCHR) voted to send the organization's representative, Mary Robinson, to investigate.[32] Canada and Guatemala were the only countries opposed to the UNCHR resolution. To the delight of Joseph Wilder, national chair of the Canada-Israel Committee, Ottawa voted against a number of other resolutions critical of Israel in April 2002. "Canada has made a conscious effort to move slightly closer to the U.S. position," he said. "We like that."[33]

The events of 9/11 gave Israel an opportunity to re-brand its suppression of Palestinians. Now part of the U.S. 'war on terror' this re-brand benefited Israel's Canadian supporters. Any sympathy Chretien had for Palestinians — compared to other prime ministers at least — was largely eclipsed by world events. Three months after 9/11 the *Ottawa Citizen* reported: "The Liberal government has quietly ordered Canadian financial institutions to freeze the assets of the radical Palestinian group Hamas, effectively declaring it a terrorist organization."[34] In November 2002 Hamas and Palestinian Islamic Jihad were officially added to Ottawa's terrorist list, which was created in the aftermath of 9/11.[35] "The Canadian government has criminalized nearly all major Palestinian political parties by designating them 'terrorist groups' under Bill C-36," which makes it illegal to support these groups in any way.[36]

The first prime minister to take office after 9/11, Paul Martin's December 2003 to January 2006 government, was more pro-Israel than Jean Chretien's. "Israel's values are Canada's values ... Shared values of democracy, the rule of law and the protection of human rights," Martin proclaimed in November 2005.[37] "Nothing will shake Canada's commitment to Israel."[38]

Israel's security fence/apartheid wall usurped a big chunk of the West Bank and cut off thousands of Palestinian farmers from their land. Still, Ottawa refused to take a clear position against the wall.[39] In December 2003, 150 countries, including all 25 European Union members, asked the International Court of Justice (ICJ) to rule on the wall's legality. Six nations opposed this: Israel, the U.S., Australia, Palau, Micronesia and the Marshall Islands. Canada abstained.[40] Foreign Affairs Minister Bill Graham said: "It's not time for the court to take this as a legal question. It's better that it remains for discussions between the parties."[41] Several months later Canada was one of only 10 countries to abstain on a resolution demanding Israel comply with the ICJ's non-binding ruling to dismantle sections of the wall.[42]

Even post-9/11 meetings between Health Canada and its Israeli counterpart took on a politically charged tone. After visiting Israel in January 2005 Public Health Minister, Carolyn Bennett, explained: "In Israel, so much is experiential. Everyone knows someone who was killed or injured in a terrorist attack, and everyone knows exactly what to do in case of emergency."[43] In contrast, Bennett did not go to Nablus and salute the "Palestinians' exceptional capacity to deal with the psychological effects of kidnapping. In Palestine everyone knows someone who has been snatched by the IDF and illegally incarcerated."

Confirming the Martin government's pro-Israel inclination, in December 2005 the *Canadian Jewish News* reported: "Canada changed its votes on three resolutions at the UN General Assembly's annual debate on the Palestinian issue, adding to Ottawa's shift toward Israel on four other resolutions last year."[44] Martin claimed Canada's pro-Israeli shift was a way to de-politicize the UN. "We will continue to press for the kinds of reform that will eliminate the politicization of the United Nations and its agencies, and in particular the annual ritual of politicized, anti-Israel resolutions."[45]

Following the Martin government came the first Harper Conservative government, which made Canada even more pro-Israel, voting against (basically) all resolutions critical of Israel. (See next chapter.)

The Left 'opposition'

The Conservatives and Liberals have one upped each other in support of Israel because there has been so little opposition from any quarter. While one might assume that the Canadian Left has long opposed Israel's Jewish supremacy, its role in advancing U.S. geopolitical interests or its status as the final frontier of European settler colonialism, unfortunately this is not the case. The Left, for decades, largely supported Zionism, which explains part of Canada's staunch support for Israel.

Initially this wasn't the case. Many leftists opposed the nationalism and imperialism associated with Zionism. In 1938 the leader of the Co-operative Commonwealth Federation (precursor to the NDP), J.S. Woodsworth, stated: "It was easy for Canadians, Americans and the British to agree to a Jewish colony, as long as it was somewhere else. Why 'pick on the Arabs' other than for 'strategic' and 'imperialistic' consideration."[46] At its 1942 convention the CCF condemned Nazi anti-Semitism but refused to endorse Zionism. "The Jewish problem can be solved only in a socialist and democratic society, which recognized no racial or class differences," explained a party resolution.[47]

But before Israel's creation the CCF officially endorsed the establishment of a Jewish state in Palestine.[48] In September 1945 new CCF leader M. J. Coldwell said the Zionist record in Palestine "in terms of both social and economic justice" spoke for itself.[49] Future CCF leader Tommy Douglas and long time federal MP Stanley Knowles, as well as a number of labour leaders, were members of the Canadian Palestine Committee (CPC), a group of prominent non-Jewish Zionists formed in December 1943. (Future External Affairs Minister Paul Martin Sr. and the premier of Alberta, Ernest C. Manning, were also members).[50] In April 1944 the CPC wrote Prime Minister Mackenzie King that it "looks forward to the day when Palestine shall ultimately become a Jewish commonwealth, and member of the British Commonwealth of Nations under the British Crown."[51]

Many CPC members' Zionism was motivated by religious belief. Both Knowles and Douglas (the 'father of Medicare') were Protestant ministers and their Zionism was partly inspired by biblical teachings. As an indication of the extent to which religion shaped Douglas his main biography is titled *Tommy Douglas: The Road to Jerusalem.*

Close to sectors of the CPC, the Canadian Congress of Labour (precursor to the Canadian Labour Congress) joined that group and the Zionist Organization of Canada to present a 1945 brief to External Affairs in support of a Jewish state.[52] Relations between Canadian labour and the Zionist union movement began two decades earlier when the Histadrut labour federation was formed in 1920.[53] For a long time the Trade Union Council for the Histadrut, a labour organization headquartered in Montreal, brought together Canadian and Israeli unions.[54] Also based in Montreal, the Canadian Association for Labour Israel (CALI) had regional offices in Toronto, Winnipeg, Ottawa and Vancouver.[55] Beginning in the mid-1920s, CALI sponsored Histradut financial campaigns in every major Canadian city.[56] To get a sense of CALI's scope, its 1960 Toronto drive raised $200,000 (more than $1 million today).[57] Published in 1958, *The Living Record of Canada's Partnership with Histadrut* explained: "The Canadian Association for Labour Israel has been supporting the constructive program of Histadrut, the Israeli labour federation, for more than three decades. Long before the State of Israel was reborn in 1948, Canadian Jews and the Canadian labour movement rendered unstinted aid to the pioneering forces then laying the foundations of an independent Jewish state."[58] Not long after Israel's creation CALI supported a Histadrut-run hostel overlooking the Gulf of Aqaba — on land Israel seized in March 1949 in breach of an armistice agreement with Egypt.[59]

More than a decade into Israel's occupation of the West Bank and Gaza strip organized labour continued to support CALI. In November 1979 the *Globe and Mail* reported that "Mr. [Max] Federman was able to draw about 1,000 union leaders, employers and friends to a $50-a-plate testimonial dinner recently. The money is to be used to build a vocational training school in Israel. Mr. Federman has been national chairman for the past 16 years of an organization of Canadian trade unionists [CALI] that supports Histadrut."[60] But Histadrut was far from a traditional labour federation. As former Israeli prime minister Golda Meir said: "Then [1928] I was put on the Histadrut Executive Committee at a time when this big labor union wasn't just a trade union organization. It was a great colonizing agency."[61] Histadrut's first Secretary-General, David Ben-Gurion, was the country's first prime minister and from 1920 to 1929 the labour federation oversaw the main Zionist military force.[62]

For decades the Histadrut owned a great deal of Israel's economy. At its height the Histadrut Workers Company was responsible for 20% of Israel's gross national product and was the second-largest employer after the state.[63] After the 1967 war the Histadrut's construction company, Solel Boneh, built most of the early settlements.[64]

Since its creation the Histadrut displayed openly racist tendencies. During British rule it undermined Jewish and Arab workers collective organizing efforts and the Histadrut prohibited Arab Israelis from joining until 1960.[65] Arabs were finally permitted to participate in Histadrut national elections in 1966. That year its name was changed from General Federation of Hebrew Workers in the Land of Israel to General Federation of Workers in the Land of Israel.[66] The Histadrut-run Workers Company did not remove Hebrew from its name until 1979.[67] In 2003 Uri Davis explained: "In the area constituting the core of the Israeli-Palestinian conflict — Zionist colonization of the land — the Histadrut continues to maintain the exclusion of its Arab members, denying them access to membership in kibbutz and moshav and other cooperative settlements. Here apartheid still rules undented."[68]

A pillar of labour Zionism, the Histadrut showcased Israel's relatively socialistic policy. In 1950, two years after more than 700,000 Palestinians were expelled from their homeland, the Histadrut's International Trade Union Department organized its first tour for Canadian labour leaders. From 1950 until at least the early 1990s, prominent Canadian union leaders visited Israel every couple of years.[69] "These tours were designed to gain good will and political support," noted the *Toronto Star*. "They resulted in many non-Jewish labour leaders becoming outspoken supporters of the state of Israel and all its actions."[70]

The Canadian Labour Congress' first Israel study mission (with high-ranking officers and staff) that did more than take a Histadrut guided tour was in the spring of 1989. That tour "visited refugee camps and, for the first time, made contact with Palestinian trade union representatives."[71] The following year, for the first time, Histadtrut delegates shared the platform at a CLC convention with Palestinian union representatives.[72] Historically, Histadtrut leaders were among a select group of honoured guests at CLC conventions, sitting next to representatives of U.S. and British unions.

Histadrut representatives helped steer CLC policy on Israel. "At every one of its annual conventions," noted a book in the late 1970s, "the CLC has passed strong pro-Israel resolutions that reflected yearly developments in the Arab-Israeli conflict."[73] The most striking example was in 1956. That year the CLC called on the Canadian government to "to lend sympathetic support to Israel's request for defensive armaments, in order that Israel may match, in quality if not quantity, the constant flow of Soviet Bloc armaments to the Arab countries, and further appeals to our government to use its good offices in urging other free Western countries to do likewise."[74] When the CLC passed that resolution Canada was already selling Israel weapons and was under pressure from Washington to ship advanced fighter jets. Moreover, has the CLC ever called on Ottawa to arm any other country?

Ottawa actively supported Israel before, during and after the June 1967 war (see Chapter 4). Despite the government's clear pro-Israel alignment NDP leader Tommy Douglas criticized Prime Minister Pearson for not backing Israel more forthrightly.[75] After the Six Day War Israel occupied the West Bank and Gaza strip as well as the Golan Heights and Egypt's Sinai. This didn't stop Tommy Douglas from telling a 1975 Histadrut gathering: "The main enmity against Israel is that she has been an affront to those nations who do not treat their people and their workers as well as Israel has treated hers."[76]

In 1975 the CLC vigorously opposed the admission of the PLO to the International Labor Organization and then condemned the General Assembly for calling Zionism a form of racism.[77] "By this act, it can justifiably be argued the UN has 'legitimized' anti-Semitism and pogroms against Jews," said CLC President Joe Morris.[78] "Canadian labour will fight all moves to implement such a [Zionism equals racism] resolution and will exercise its influence to prevent further extensions of the resolution."[79]

It may seem like ancient history to unions that have joined the growing "boycott, divestment and sanctions" (BDS) campaign but in September 1977 the CLC called on Ottawa to block companies from acquiescing to an Arab boycott designed to pressure Israel to return land it captured in 1967.[80] Similarly, the NDP denounced the Trudeau government for its response to the economic boycott. Winnipeg NDP MP David Orlikow said: "It is regrettable it has taken so long for the government to make any kind of statement on a very basic principle."[81] He called for Trudeau to give "favorable consideration" to legislation blocking Canadian companies from participating in the Arab boycott.[82]

The election of rightist Prime Minister Menachem Begin in 1977 and Israel's full-scale invasion of Lebanon in 1982 weakened its support among organized labour. Still, the CLC leadership generally supported Israel's actions. Before the 1982 invasion the CLC noted that "the establishment of an independent and sovereign government in Lebanon, which is capable of preventing that country from being used to launch terrorist attacks against its neighbors, is the key to peace in the Middle East."[83] "Terrorist attacks" was not a reference to Israel's 1978 invasion of Lebanon or its repeated cross-border incursions, only PLO attacks on Israel. The CLC condemned the civilian casualties caused by Israel's 1982 invasion of Lebanon but largely blamed them on the PLO. "The PLO has brought Israeli retribution to Lebanon. It is impossible for the CLC to ignore that it has brought much more. Its major legacy has been the civil war in 1975 and 1976, when 60,000 people were killed."[84] The CLC report titled *An Effective Peace in the Middle East* continued: "The Israeli invasion of Lebanon may have broken the power of the PLO, enabling the Palestinian people to secure constructive representation, and this outcome would be welcomed by the Canadian Labour Congress."[85]

An Effective Peace in the Middle East also detailed the union federation's position on the Arab-Israeli conflict more generally: "Arab countries and peoples must categorically accept Israel's right to exist and live within secure and recognized boundaries. Continued violence against Israel is totally incompatible with such acceptance. For its part, Israel must honour the Camp David Accords, as it did in withdrawing from the [Egyptian] Sinai, by recognizing the legitimate rights of the Palestinian people and their just requirements. That the principal requirements will remain a national homeland for the Palestinians is obvious to the CLC, and it is the view of the CLC that the hatred of the PLO terrorist organization for Israel is in fact a major impediment in the way of the creation of a Palestinian homeland."[86]

In July 1983, the NDP echoed the CLC's statement calling on Arab countries and the PLO to recognize Israel's "right to live in peace with its neighbours within secure and recognized boundaries. ... The failure to extend this recognition has been, for Israel, a justifiable barrier to its engaging in direct negotiations with representatives of the Palestinians."[87] According to the NDP and CLC version of history, Israel's 15-year-old illegal occupation of Palestinian lands was motivated by a dislike for the PLO.

In 1985 a Senate committee report rebuked Israel's 1982 invasion/occupation of Lebanon and provided mild support for the PLO. "The CLC was the only non-Jewish organization to condemn the Senate report," noted the *Globe and Mail*.[88] The report stopped short of calling for Canada to join most UN members and recognize the PLO as Palestinians' legitimate voice (instead of Israeli backed "village leagues" designed to divide the rural and urban populations).[89] A self-described "Catholic Zionist," CLC president Dennis McDermott explained: "I severely criticized the report on the Middle East by the Canadian Senate Standing Committee on Foreign Affairs, which attempted to legitimize the PLO. I said then that the committee was guilty of 'an exercise in bad judgment and even worse taste,' and that the senators were seriously misguided in their report, which 'tries as hard as it can to portray the PLO as a democratic charity, busy building kindergartens ...' I made the further point 'that it was the PLO that gave the world airline terrorism.'... I take considerable pride in my long-standing role in Canada and abroad as a spokesman on behalf of the legitimate aspirations of the state of Israel, and as a critic of the PLO and its misguided friends."[90] Israel's labour movement showed its gratitude to McDermott. His portrait hangs in a Histadrut trade school library named in his honour.[91]

Since the mid-1980s the broad Left has made great strides in opposing Israeli policy. But the Left is still far from unanimously antagonistic towards Israeli policy in Palestine, its domestic racism or its belligerence in the region. Canadian unions purchase $20 million worth of State of Israel Bonds annually.[92] Founded in 1996-97, the Israel Bonds' Canadian labour division holds tribute dinners to honour union leaders.[93] Economics is the main motivation for acquiring Israel Bonds but there is also "a historical bond between Israel and the unions," explained Lawrence Waller, executive vice-president of State of Israel Bonds Canada.[94] "We in Israel promote [to Canadian unions] the fact that 100 percent of our public works are unionized."[95]

In 2000 Hamilton's Jewish National Fund dedicated its Negev Dinner to Enrico and Joe Mancinelli from the Laborers' International Union of North America (LIUNA). The union's pension fund began investing in State of Israel Bonds in the early 1980s and in 1999 Joe Mancinelli visited Israel to see construction and infrastructure projects financed by Israel Bonds.[96] "They have a longstanding relationship with and support for the state of Israel," explained JNF Hamilton chairperson Tom Weisz.[97] For its part, the

Quebec Federation of Labour's Solidarity Fund participated in a provincial business delegation to Israel in the fall of 2008.[98]

NDP MPs still tour the region with pro-Israel groups. (Could one imagine NDP MPs visiting South Africa with pro-apartheid groups?) In October 2004 Winnipeg NDP MPs Judy Wasylycia-Leis and Pat Martin went on a Canada-Israel Committee sponsored trip. "It was an incredible experience for me," Wasylycia-Leis explained. "It was an opportunity to see first-hand the impact of terrorism on the lives of the people of Israel. We also got a good sense of what the fence is all about. Israel certainly has the right to defend itself from suicide bombers."[99] For his part, Martin said: "That fence shows a lot of restraint on Israel's part. If I were living there, I don't think I would be able to exhibit such restraint."[100] On another occasion Martin argued: "the fence intrudes onto only 15 percent of West Bank territory. If it were considered to be a new and permanent barrier, why would Israel's Prime Minister, Ariel Sharon, settle for such a modest gain? Even the most charitable of Mr. Sharon's critics accuse him of harbouring much more expansive territorial ambitions."[101] Notwithstanding the NDP MPs, the vast majority of UN members and the International Court of Justice condemned the fence/barrier/apartheid wall that reaches several kilometres into the West Bank and cuts thousands of Palestinian farmers off from their lands.

In mid-2008 the NDP initially opposed but then supported the Harper government when it made Canada the first country to withdraw from the second World Conference Against Racism, Racial Discrimination, Xenophobia and Related Intolerance ("Durban II"). This was to the delight of the Israeli government, which was the second country to pull out (criticism of Zionism at Durban I was deemed "anti-Semitic"). For her part, Green party leader Elizabeth May applauded the Conservative's decision. "It's [antiracism conference] become a mockery. I can't think of any other UN process that I would avoid [other than] that one."[102]

During Israel's December 2008/January 2009 assault on Gaza Manitoba NDP Justice Minister Dave Chomiak took part in a Stand With Israel event in Winnipeg alongside Conservative and Liberal MPs. Chomiak told those gathered that "The enemy and the fear are terrorists who know no limits."[103] He was referring to Hamas operatives with their homemade rockets and machine guns, not the U.S./Canada equipped IDF responsible for a hundred times more deaths than the few killed in Israel.

A month later the B.C. NDP demonstrated a similar deference to pro-Israel groups. In March 2009 B.C. NDP candidate Mable Elmore was lambasted for having used the term "Zionist" five years earlier to describe pro-war activists in her union. NDP leader Carole James immediately criticized the comment.

But there has been a significant reversal of leftwing support for Israel. The Canadian Left is slowly catching up to the rest of the world in seeing the fundamental injustice of Zionism. Palestinian Canadian activists, alongside many Jews, have worked tirelessly to make opposition to Zionism a central part of the Left's political culture. This work has paid off with larger and larger demonstrations against Israeli policies. This will be discussed further in the last chapter.

Chapter 8
The world's most pro-Israel country

The trajectory of this country's foreign policy has been clear: The culmination of six decades of one-sided support, and two years into the Stephen Harper government, Canada was (at least diplomatically) the most pro-Israel country in the world.

In January 2008 the *Globe and Mail* reported that "by refusing to condemn the building [of illegal settlements near Jerusalem] at Harhoma, [Foreign Affairs Minister Maxime] Mr. Bernier appeared to have made Canadian foreign policy the most pro-Israeli in the world. Last week, even the United States, usually Israel's staunchest ally, slammed the new construction here."[1]

A year and a half later Israel began barring some North Americans with Palestinian-sounding names entry through Tel Aviv's Ben Gurion Airport. Forced to reroute through a land-border crossing that connects the West Bank with Jordan, their passports were stamped "Palestinian Authority only," which prevented them from entering Israel proper. The Obama Administration objected to Israel's move to discriminate against American citizens of Palestinian origin. There was no protest from Ottawa even though *Time* magazine and *Haaretz* ran lengthy articles focusing on Palestinian Canadian businessmen harmed by this policy. "Although some of the most high-profile cases of individuals being turned away involve Canadian citizens, the Harper government has, so far, made no protest."[2]

In fact, by fall 2008, the Conservatives publicly proclaimed that Canada was the most pro-Israel country in the world.[3] So did Israeli officials. After meeting Canada's foreign affairs minister, four other Conservative ministers and Liberal leader Michael Ignatieff in July 2009, Israel's Foreign Minister Avigdor Lieberman, who has openly called for the expulsion of Israeli Arabs, commented: "It's hard to find a country friendlier to Israel than Canada these days.

Members both of the coalition and the opposition are loyal friends to us, both with regard to their worldview and their estimation of the situation in everything related to the Middle East, North Korea, Iran, Sudan and Somalia. No other country in the world has demonstrated such full understanding of us…"

"Canada is so friendly that there was no need to convince or explain anything to anyone. We had amiable talks in a supportive atmosphere; we seriously discussed the problems existing in the world. We need allies like this in the international arena."[4]

For defining Canadian policy as "we support Israel no matter what it does" B'Nai Brith international bestowed Harper with its Presidential Gold Medallion for Humanitarianism.[5] The first Canadian to receive the award, Harper joined David Ben Gurion, and U.S. presidents John F. Kennedy and Harry S. Truman. For its part, the Canadian Jewish Congress gave Harper its "prestigious Saul Hayes Human Rights award, named for a former CJC executive director, the first time it's been given to a sitting PM."[6]

In a blatant example of Canadian support for Israeli aggression the Conservatives defended Israel's summer 2006 military invasion, Israel's fifth, of Lebanon. When Stephen Harper told reporters that Israel's assault on Lebanon was a "measured response" to Hezbollah incursions, he probably regretted it.[7] Two days later, Israel wiped out an entire Lebanese-Canadian family, including four children aged 1 to 8. Harper's comment brought the kind of publicity even a staunchly pro-Israel prime minister did not like. But with 1,100 (mostly civilian) Lebanese dead and much of the country's infrastructure destroyed, the Conservatives continued to endorse Israel's aggression. Three months after the conclusion of hostilities, Harper vetoed a 55-member Francophonie statement that "'deplored' the effect of the month-long conflict on the Lebanese civilians it endangered."[8] For Harper the statement was too one-sided, even if the 33-day war caused more than ten times the deaths on the Lebanese side in a country with a little more than half of Israel's population. Even Lebanon's staunchly pro-western, anti-Hezbollah Prime Minister, Fuad Saniora, criticized Ottawa for supporting Israel's aggression.[9]

During its bombing of Lebanon, Israel destroyed a UN compound, killing Canadian Major Paeta Hess-Von Kruedener. At the time of the bombing Harper publicly questioned the UN for keeping its forces in the war zone and demanded answers. When a UN inquiry concluded that on the day of the fatal bombing, Hezbollah fighters were nowhere near the UN post the "pro-military" Conservative government ignored the report.[10] In fact, *Embassy Magazine* reported that Israel's ambassador, Alan Baker, said: "there was no high-level push for accountability from Canada."[11]

After the war, Ottawa strengthened its relations with the Lebanese groups least resistant to Israel's aggression. Canada followed Washington's lead in arming the Lebanese army as a counterweight to Hezbollah's military force.[12] Ottawa also openly supported the pro-Western anti-Hezbollah faction during the political crisis that followed the war. Foreign Affairs Minister Peter MacKay said: "Hezbollah is a cancer on Lebanon, which is destroying stability and democracy within its boundaries."[13] A couple months later MacKay called Hezbollah the "Taliban on steroids."[14] For his part, Public Safety Minister Stockwell Day added, the "stated intent of Hezbollah is to annihilate Jewish people."[15] Jason Kenney echoed this statement in September 2009, saying Hezbollah is "motivated by a profound anti-Semitism."[16]

Despite Kenney and Day's claims, Hezbollah was created in response to Israel's 1982-2000 occupation of Lebanon and its pronouncements suggest it is largely concerned with Israel's occupation of Arab lands.

This extreme demonization of Hezbollah — "Lebanon's largest political party and most potent armed force" — did not begin with Harper.[17] In December 2002 Jean Chretien buckled under pro-Israel pressure and added Hezbollah to its list of terrorist organizations, which made it illegal to support it in any way.[18] This undercut the political potential of Canada's large Lebanese diaspora. The terrorist label also adds a further barrier to serious public discussion about the region. Prominent individuals connected to Hezbollah in any way can be dubbed 'terrorist supporter', which the media has done on a number of occasions, including when a Bloc Quebecois MP forwarded an e-mail to parliamentarians with a link to an article supporting Hezbollah and Hamas.[19]

Barely mentioned in the media, Harper also strengthened relations with the Jordanian monarchy, a government amenable to Israel. In the summer of 2008 Jordan became the first Middle Eastern country (after Israel) to sign a Free Trade Agreement with Ottawa. It was also the first Arab country to sign an FTA with Washington. *Embassy Magazine* described the geopolitics driving the agreement: "Trade Deal Would Be Reward for Jordan's Moderate Stance."[20]

Widely viewed as the lobby power driving Canada's "free" trade agenda, the head of the Canadian Council of Chief Executives, Thomas d'Aquino, sent a letter to Harper calling on Ottawa to negotiate a trade agreement with Jordan. "Jordan is a very moderate country, a country that is led by a leader that has the right kind of ideas on what kind of Middle East we should be trying to build."[21] D'Aquino added, "Jordan does have a peace agreement with Israel and, in my opinion, every little bit helps."[22] The king's undemocratic and repressive nature was rarely mentioned; instead the focus was on its "good governance" and "moderate" nature.[23]

Compared to Jordan, Iran is quite democratic. But, it is perceived as hostile to Western elite interests, which is why Harper's Conservatives laid the groundwork for a U.S./Israeli attack on Iran. Throughout his time in office Canadian naval vessels have run provocative manoeuvres off Iran's coast and Ottawa has been accused of spying for the U.S.

"Canada attacks Iran's record on human rights," noted an October 2009 *National Post* article.[24] Ottawa-lead efforts to censure Iran for its human rights violations were part of a plan to destabilize the Islamic Republic. In November 2007 the *Ottawa Citizen* reported: "In what one western diplomat described as a 'division of labour', among western governments to keep up the pressure on Iran, the big European powers and the United States lead western efforts to convince Iran to roll back its nuclear program while Canada has spearheaded resolutions denouncing the way Iran treats huge numbers of its people."[25]

In January 2007 Foreign Affairs Minister Peter MacKay said: "The regime in Tehran cannot be allowed to acquire nuclear weapons."[26] McKay's comment was made in Israel, a regional rival of Iran that possesses nuclear weapons. New Foreign Affairs Minister Lawrence Cannon echoed this statement in mid-2009: "A nuclear threat against Israel is a threat against us all." He continued, "(The Israelis) were very concerned and worried about Iran acquiring nuclear weapons. We share that concern."[27]

For his part, Harper told the *Wall Street Journal* in February 2009: "It concerns me that we have a regime with both an ideology that is obviously evil, combined with the desire to procure technology to act on that ideology... my government is a very strong supporter of the state of Israel and considers the Iranian threats to be absolutely unacceptable and beyond the pale."[28]

But isn't it Israel that possesses nuclear weapons and threatens to attack Iran, not the other way around? While Ottawa considers Iran's nuclear energy program a major threat, Israel's atomic bombs have not provoked similar condemnation.

At a number of International Atomic Energy Agency (IAEA) meetings the Harper government abstained on votes asking Israel to place its nuclear weapons program under IAEA controls (the same controls demanded of Iran). In September 2009 Ottawa condemned as "unbalanced" an IAEA resolution calling on Israel to join the Nuclear Non-Proliferation Treaty and have its nuclear facilities inspected.[29] Ottawa tried to block the vote. Ultimately, 100 countries supported the resolution while Israel opposed it. Canada, India, Georgia and the U.S. abstained.[30] Three years earlier Canada introduced a no action motion that blocked an IAEA resolution labelling Israel's nuclear capabilities a threat. "The draft resolution, which also called upon Israel to join the Nuclear Non-proliferation Treaty, was blocked from going to a vote yesterday by the Canadian delegate."[31] Similarly, in December 1997 the General Assembly called on Israel to sign the nonproliferation Treaty. Israel voted no and Canada abstained.

(For a more thorough discussion of Canadian policy in the wider Middle East see my *Black Book of Canadian Foreign Policy*.)

The Harper government worked hard to strengthen Israel's position vis-a-vis the Palestinians. "Canada vetoes key UN motion on refugees," read a *Globe and Mail* headline a month after the Conservatives took power.[32] In March 2006 Canada joined the U.S. "as the only two countries to oppose a resolution that called on Israel to allow Palestinian refugee women and children to return to Israeli territory. The vote was 41-2 in favour of the non-binding resolution, passed by the UN Economic and Social Council (UN-ESC)."[33]

In the summer of 2006 Canada opposed a UN Human Rights Council resolution condemning Israel's offensive into Gaza and calling on Israel to release Palestinian officials it illegally arrested. Twenty-nine countries voted for the resolution, 11 against and five abstained. Ottawa claimed the resolution didn't take Israel's security concerns into account.[34]

In January 2008 Canada was one of seven countries to vote against the April 2009 World Conference Against Racism (dubbed "Durban II") and was among 41 General Assembly members to oppose allocating $6.8 million (US) for preparatory meetings.[35] A few months later Canada was the first country to withdraw from

Durban II. "When Canada left Durban II it said it would not be 'party to an anti-Semitic, anti-western hate fest dressed up as an antiracism conference.'"[36] Israel, the second country to pull out, was delighted. Foreign Minister Tzipi Livni said: "The Canadian decision, at this early stage, undoubtedly will shake the entire foundation of those wishing to repeat the 2001 Durban Conference" where it was alleged that criticism of Zionism was "anti-Semitic".[37] Additionally, Immigration Minister Jason Kenney said: "We [the Canadian International Development Agency] will not subsidize NGOs to attend the Durban conference."[38] (Defending Israel was only part of the Harper government's motivation for pulling out of the antiracism conference. They also had little interest in discussing the dispossession of First Nations, colonialism or the African slave trade. Claiming the conference was anti-Semitic was the only politically palatable justification for withdrawing. In fact, Israel was barely on the agenda.)

In March 2009 the *Canadian Jewish News* reported: "The United Nations Human Rights Council ... approved five anti-Israel resolutions in which it took issue with Israel's continued settlement activity, its treatment of West Bank Palestinians and its January military operation in Gaza. Canada was the sole country to object to all the resolutions. They were joined in one instance by the Netherlands, Germany and Italy, who opposed the resolution against Israeli military activity in Gaza."[39]

Two days after Harper won a minority government in January 2006, Hamas won Canadian-monitored and facilitated legislative elections in Palestine. Soon after assuming power Harper made Canada the first country (after Israel) to cut its assistance to the Palestinian Authority.[40] "The response of Canada, under Harper, to this democratic result was to cut aid to the starving and besieged Palestinians. Harper was following senior advisor to [Israeli Prime Minister] Ariel Sharon, Dov Wiseglass, who announced a plan to 'put Palestinians on a diet.'"[41]

Palestinians were not happy about being forced to "diet." Canada's Representative Office in Ramallah "was riddled with bullets ... shortly after Canada became the first country to impose sanctions against Palestinians in 2006."[42] The aid cutoff, which was designed to sow division within Palestinian society, had devastating social effects. "Open warfare among Gazan families a byproduct of aid freeze," explained a *Globe and Mail* headline.[43]

Ostensibly the aid cut-off was due to Hamas' refusal to recognize Israel, yet Canada has not severed relations with numerous Likud governments, even though it is a party that does not recognize Palestinians' right to a state.[44] Harper explained: "Future assistance to any new Palestinian government will be reviewed against that government's commitment to the principles of non-violence, recognition of Israel and acceptance of previous agreements and obligations."[45] But support for Israel was never made contingent on "non violence" or an end to settlement construction.

In March 2007 political factions representing more than 90% of the Palestinian Legislative Council established a unity government. Still, the Conservatives shunned the new government. "It's our policy to have no contact with members of the government or deputy ministers — that's what we're suggesting," said Daniel Dugas, Foreign Affairs Minister Peter MacKay's director of communications.[46] The Conservatives claimed to speak regularly (like the Israelis) with Palestinian president Mahmoud Abbas.

When the unity government's information minister traveled to Ottawa on a global peace tour in March 2007 Foreign Affairs Minister Peter MacKay refused to meet him. Mustafa Barghouti, who represented a secular party, explained: "I think the Canadian government is the only government that is taking such a position, except for Israel. Even the United States has sent its consul general [in Jerusalem, Jacob Walles,] to meet with the Palestinian finance minister [Salam Fayyad]."[47] Barghouti had already met the foreign ministers of Sweden and Norway, the Secretary-General of the UN and U.S. Secretary of State Condoleezza Rice.[48]

Ottawa wanted to sow division within Palestinian society by destroying the unity government. Once Hamas officials were ousted from the Palestinian Authority in 2007 Ottawa restarted diplomatic relations and financial support. "Canada to restore relations with new, Hamas-free Palestinian Authority," explained the *Globe and Mail*.[49] "The Government of Canada welcomes the leadership of President Abbas and Prime Minister [Salam] Fayyad in establishing a government that Canada and the rest of the international community can work with," explained MacKay after the unity government's collapse.[50] "In light of the new Palestinian government's commitment to non-violence, recognition of Israel, and acceptance of previous agreements and obligations, and in recognition of the opportunity for a renewal of peace efforts, Canada will provide assistance to the new Palestinian government."[51]

With Palestinian society divided and a more compliant authority in control of the West Bank, the Canadian International Development Agency contributed $8 million "in direct support to the new government."[52] Part of this aid was directed towards creating a Palestinian police force "to ensure that the PA maintains control of the West Bank against Hamas, [Canadian ambassador to Israel Jon] Allen said."[53] U.S. Lt. General Keith Dayton, in charge of organizing the 7,500 member Palestinian force, never admitted he strengthened Fatah against Hamas but to justify his program Dayton argued that Iran and Syria funded and armed Hamas.[54] Dayton said that "we must make sure that the moderate [Palestinian] forces will not be erased."[55]

Washington and Ottawa pushed for war between Hamas and Fatah.[56] A senior figure in the Israeli intelligence establishment explained: "Washington did not want a unity government. It wanted Fatah to wreck it and it sent Dayton to create and train a force that could overthrow Hamas. When Hamas preempts it, everyone cries foul, claiming it's a military putsch by Hamas — but who did the putsch?"[57]

In January 2007 Foreign Affairs Minister Peter MacKay offered an immediate $1.2 million for Dayton's mission.[58] A fifth of Dayton's initial staff were Canadian and in Jerusalem U.S. Secretary of State Condoleezza Rice said Dayton "has a Canadian counterpart with whom he works very closely."[59] Foreign Affairs Minister Maxime Bernier met Dayton when he traveled to Israel in January 2008 and by April 2009 Dayton's military training force in the West Bank reportedly included nine Canadians, 16 Americans, three Brits and one Turk.[60]

Palestinian security forces were primarily trained at the U.S.-built International Police Training Center in Jordan. In October 2009 the *Wall Street Journal* reported, "[Palestinian] recruits are trained in Jordan by Jordanian police, under the supervision of American, Canadian and British officers."[61] While the number of Canadians in Jordan was not publicly available it was reported that Canada helped train tens of thousands of Iraqi police at that facility.[62]

The top Canadian on Dayton's force, Colonel Chris Simonds, described the tension between Israel's medium-term goal to offload the administration of its occupation to compliant Palestinians and the short-term necessity to dominate. "Our goal is to assist the PA in carrying out its obligations under the road map." But, "almost every night they [Israel] conduct raids somewhere in Area A [the area supposedly controlled by the Palestinian Authority]," Simonds explained to the *Globe and Mail* in April 2009. "I understand the Israeli concerns," he added. "They get information on what might be a terrorist plan and they have to act." Simonds, however, would prefer to see the Palestinian force do Israel's dirty work. "It would be better, though, if they [Israel] gave the information to the PA and let them handle things," he said. "But they're not willing to do this, at least not yet."[63]

Bolstering Fatah to weaken Hamas was the impetus for Dayton's mission but the broader aim was to build a force to patrol Israel's occupation. "During the [late 2008] attack on Gaza," Noam Chomsky explained, "there was concern that there might be protests in the West Bank, but they were put down; they were put down by an army run by General Keith Dayton, U.S. General; trained and armed by Jordan and Israel, which is imposed in order to control the population of the West Bank."[64] Chomsky should have added Canada and maybe a few European countries to his list of trainers. In June 2008 the Conservatives boasted that "Canada is a strong supporter of Palestinian security system reform, particularly through our contribution to the mission of Lt. General Keith Dayton, the U.S. security coordinator, and to the European Union Police Coordinating Office for Palestinian Police Support."[65]

Canada's contribution to the Dayton mission was part of a $300 million Palestinian "aid" package that began in December 2007.[66] According to a March 2008 Public Safety Canada press release, "a significant component [of the $300 million will be] devoted to security, including policing and public order capacity-building. This five year commitment will go towards the creation of a democratic, accountable, and viable Palestinian state that lives in peace and security alongside Israel."[67]

But does anything close to a "viable Palestinian state" exist? Is Israel allowing it to be created? Growing Jewish settlements, Israeli bypass roads and the apartheid barrier all make a Palestinian state far from realistic in the short to medium term. Yet Canadian officials pretend that Israel is working towards a Palestinian state.

Another part of this "not unconditional" $300 million in financial aid to the PA for "nation building" included "educational programs to combat hatred and incitement" against Israel.[68] A Palestinian-based NGO observer noted that Canadian aid to Palestine "ultimately works to support [Israeli] military security at the price of [Palestinian] human security."[69] Canadian officials were open about it. A Saint John *Telegraph-Journal* headline explained: "Canada's aid to Palestine benefits Israel, foreign affairs minister says."[70] In January 2008 Minister Bernier said: "We are doing that [providing aid to the PA] because we want Israel to be able to live in peace and security with its neighbours."[71]

Since the Oslo negotiations in 1993 Ottawa has provided hundreds of millions in aid to Palestine in large part to support U.S./Israeli moves to create a Palestinian security/government apparatus to oversee Israel's occupation.

In Gaza, Israel's occupation turned into a blockade. For dozens of months, Israel reduced food and medicine from entering the tiny coastal territory to a fraction of what was needed. Yet, the Harper government refused to criticize the siege. Canada was the only country at the UN Human Rights Council (UNHRC) to vote against a January 2008 resolution that called for "urgent international action to put an immediate end to Israel's siege of Gaza." It was adopted by 30 votes with 15 abstentions.[72]

The Conservatives were quick to congratulate Israel for any pause in its blockade. In January 2009 International Development Minister Bev Oda proclaimed: "We commend Israel's decision to facilitate the delivery of humanitarian assistance [to Gaza] through a temporary ceasefire."[73] A day after Oda's announcement, Israeli forces fired on a UN convoy during a ceasefire, killing a Palestinian aid worker. There was no follow-up statement from Oda condemning Israel's actions.[74]

Canada further legitimized Israel's siege of Gaza by directly participating in it. In early 2009 Canada joined the Gaza Counter-Arms Smuggling Initiative alongside Israel, Spain, France, Germany, Norway, Denmark, Italy and the U.S.. "By addressing arms smuggling and the continued threat of terrorism through this initiative, Canada continues to contribute to a sustainable peace in the region, along with its international partners," explained Foreign Affairs Minister Lawrence Cannon.[75] "We look forward to continuing work with our partners on the program of action to coordinate efforts to stop the flow of arms, ammunition and related material into the Gaza Strip."[76] Cannon, of course, was not referring to IDF weaponry that has killed thousands in Gaza.

A March 2008 Israeli incursion into Gaza claimed more than 120 lives.[77] In response, 33 members of the 47-seat UNHRC voted for a resolution accusing Israel of war crimes. Thirteen countries abstained and only Canada opposed that resolution.[78]

Israel unleashed a much greater assault on Gaza in December 2008. Ottawa wholeheartedly supported Israel's 22-day campaign that left more than 1,200 Palestinians dead. "Canada's position has been well known from the very beginning. Hamas is a terrorist group. Israel defended itself," Minister Cannon explained.[79] Ottawa even justified Israel's killing of 40 Palestinian civilians at a UN-run school. "Israelis hit school, Ottawa blames Hamas" noted a *Toronto Star* headline.[80] Junior Foreign Affairs Minister Peter Kent said: "We really don't have complete details yet, other than the fact that we know that Hamas has made a habit of using civilians and civilian infrastructure as shields for their terrorist activities, and that would seem to be the case again today."[81] Kent added that Hamas "bears the full responsibility for the deepening humanitarian tragedy. .. In many ways, Hamas behaves as if they are trying to have more of their people killed to make a terrible terrorist point."[82] Presumably the "terrible terrorist point" was that the Israeli army brutally murders Palestinian civilians. It was not hard to prove.

When Eva Bartlett, a Canadian humanitarian worker in Gaza, told Canada's mission in Tel Aviv she was "being shot at by Israeli soldiers on the other side of the border fence" they justified Israel's actions.[83] Her blog reports: "Jordie Elms, the Canadian attaché in the Tel Aviv office, informed us that 'Israel has declared the one km area along the border to be a 'closed military zone' and added that humanitarian and aid workers need to 'know the risk of being in a closed area.'"[84]

Compared to Ottawa's cheerleading most of the world was hostile to Israel's actions. Most countries criticized the killing of civilians. In solidarity with Gaza, Venezuela expelled Israel's ambassador at the start of the bombardment and then broke off all diplomatic relations two weeks later. Israel didn't need to worry since Ottawa was prepared to help out. "Israel's interests in Caracas will now be represented by the Canadian Embassy," explained the *Jerusalem Post* (Ottawa had been "doing this for Israel in Cuba" since 1973).[85] In August 2009 the Canadian embassy in Caracas began providing visas to Venezuelans traveling to Israel.[86] Canada officially became Israel, at least in Venezuela.

Canada's ardent support for Israel's assault on Gaza did not go unnoticed around the world. In Tehran the Iranian Foreign Ministry summoned Canada's chargé d'affaires James Carrick. "Canada's negative vote [at the UN Human Rights Council] on the resolution means turning a blind eye to the Israeli crimes committed against Palestinian civilians and is a blatant violation of basic human rights," explained an Iranian Foreign Ministry statement.[87] "Ottawa provoque L'ire du monde Arabe," read a January 2009 *Le Devoir* headline.[88] The Palestinian Authority and 14 other ambassadors in Ottawa demanded Foreign Affairs Minister Cannon meet them to discuss Canada's support for Israel's assault on Gaza. Ottawa's position also prompted the biggest pro-Palestinian demonstrations ever in Canada. (See final chapter.)

The Harper government's shift towards almost always supporting Israel at the UN prompted some consternation among the foreign-policy establishment. "Canada's voting pattern on all resolutions concerning Israel have clearly marked the Canadian government as standing on its own," a 2008 Senate committee report explained. "Diplomats in Geneva pointed out that Canada has now voted four times against resolutions on its own while Canada's traditional allies have instead generally chosen to abstain from the vote."[89]

Broadly supportive of the Harper government's position, the Senate committee worried that Canada's unflinching support for Israel hurt its credibility on other issues. "Canadian diplomats in Geneva noted that Canada's recent isolation has had a negative impact on its ability to influence other matters. The OIC [Organization of Islamic Countries] and other states have retaliated against Canada on other issues as a result of some of the principled [pro-Israeli] stances that Canada has adopted on issues surrounding Israel."[90]

One wonders what further price Canadians will pay for their government's actions. Certainly, every Canadian who believes in the principles of human rights, even-handedness and peacekeeping in foreign affairs should be embarrassed by our government's record.

Chapter 9
Maintaining support for Israel

What is the explanation for Canada's one-sided pro-Israel foreign policy? Three decades ago the answer may have been that it reflected the popular will, but how about today when more and more people view Israel as a dangerous, destabilizing influence on world peace? (One poll of 27 countries around the world in 2007 rated Israel more negatively than any other, including Iran, North Korea and the U.S.[1]) Among the reasons for the overwhelming pro-Israel bias in Canadian institutions are the influence of religion, threats of being called anti-Semitic, the strength of the Israeli lobby and the power of the U.S. empire.

With friends like these — Canadian Chistian Zionists

Among the most important "friends" of Israel are adherents to certain interpretations of Christianity. Biblical literalists have spurred popular sympathy for Israel and motivated Canadian political parties to ignore the suffering of Palestinians.

In mid-2006 preeminent U.S. Christian Zionist John Hagee spoke on the outskirts of Toronto. Publicized entirely through Christian broadcasters and church bulletins 2,000 evangelicals attended.[2] The next year Hagee held his 25th night to honour Israel at his home church in San Antonio. Twenty-fifth anniversary events were held in cities across North America including Toronto where they raised $500,000 for Israel.[3]

In charge of the John Hagee Ministries in Canada, Charles McVety is Canada's leading Christian Zionist. An influential Conservative Party operative, McVety leads the Defend Marriage Coalition, Ottawa's Institute for Canadian Values and Christians United for Israel (Canada). "Israel is the number one family-values issue," said McVety, explaining the connection between opposition to gay marriage and abortion and support for Israel. "Where does marriage come from? God. Where does the Bible come from? Israel. The first family of Christianity — Jesus, Mary, and Joseph — were all Jewish. Israel is the source of everything we have."[4]

A busy man, McVety presided over Canada Christian College in North York Ontario. To honour Israel's 60th birthday Canada Christian College created a department to study Israel. The department "is a powerful symbol of the extraordinary working relationship and devotion of the evangelical movement with the modern State of Israel and the Jewish people throughout the world," McVety explained.[5] "We hope that the introduction of this Chair will serve as a catalyst for other Christian schools, both in Canada and abroad, to create similar departments devoted to the study of modern Israel."[6] The department's first chair was B'nai Brith's executive director Frank Dimant who is an unabashed supporter of all things Israel. Standing next to Dimant, McVety declared: "We will stand together until Messiah comes."[7]

Canada Christian College also held a birthday party in May 2008 when close to 1,000 people gathered to celebrate Israel's 60th.[8] The Christians United for Israel/B'nai Brith sponsored event included cabinet minister Jason Kenney (who read a letter from Stephen Harper), Israel's Consul General, Amir Gissin, and Ontario MPP Monte Kwinter (who read a letter from Premier Dalton McGuinty).

Demonstrating the precarious alliance between Jewish and Evangelical Zionists, in the early 90s Canada Christian College had its accreditation withheld partly because of the Canadian Jewish Congress.[9] The CJC claimed some of the college's courses were designed to convert Jews. The seven-year dispute ended after the college closed its controversial Jewish studies department and dismissed two faculty members.[10]

To highlight Israel's 60th, the pastor of the First Nations Family Worship Centre in Winnipeg launched World Indigenous Nations for Israel.[11] Rev. Raymond McLean told Israel birthday revellers in Winnipeg: "We are going to be celebrating all year, because the Jewish people got their land back that God had promised them."[12] McLean, who had been to Israel more than eight times, said: "I believe that since the Jewish people are God's chosen people, we have to stand with them."[13]

Canadian Christians regularly make political pilgrimages to Israel. Several months after the outbreak of the second intifada, in February 2001, 80 Christian activists boarded an El Al flight to "bring a blessing for the new olim [immigrants]" and the State of Israel.[14] Executive director of Christians for Israel (Canada) Dean Bye explained: "We want to stand in solidarity with Israel; we want them to know there are Canadian Christians who pray for them and who stand with them."[15]

Thirty supporters of Bridges for Peace (Canada), an international organization that brings Jews from Eastern Europe to Israel, joined the delegation. Two weeks prior to this delegation Rev. John Howson, a Bridges for Peace representative, led 24 pastors on a tour of Israel. Howson split his time between Winnipeg and his office in Jerusalem.[16] In June 2008 Howson, then national director of Bridges For Peace, said: "We aren't going to fall for the Palestinian verbiage ... We know that only Israel and the Jews will safeguard our freedom of access to our religious sites. It seems strange for the Palestinians to be demanding more liberties when Prime Minister [Ehud] Barak offered them east Jerusalem and sovereignty on the Temple Mount and they turned it down."[17]

These missions, which strengthen support for expansionist policies among Israelis, are largely designed for the Canadian public. In March 2003, 20 leading evangelical authors, television personalities and educators went on a week-long solidarity mission to Israel. Charles McVety said the mission was to "educate evangelicals why, according to scripture, they must support Israel."[18] Upon returning, mission delegates were expected to "stand up and support Israel."[19]

The delegation included representatives from evangelical TV stations in Winnipeg (Trinity TV), Lethbridge (Miracle Channel), Burlington (Crossroads Christian Communications) and Vancouver (Now TV). A Toronto-based author who has sold millions of copies of more than 20 books on Biblical prophecy, Grant Jeffrey, said mission participants "believe Israel needs to be supported as a vibrant democracy in a sea of dictatorships … We want to commit and say we stand with Israel shoulder to shoulder."[20]

Israel's Tourist Office, along with McVety and El Al Airlines, organized this March 2003 tour for media personalities.[21] Israel promotes its "holy" credentials to garner political support among Bible literalists and to strengthen its tourism industry, one of the country's leading sources of foreign currency earnings.[22] Tourism plummeted with the outbreak of the second intifada but then Christians "saved the industry," Israeli Tourism Minister Benny Elon told the *Canadian Jewish News* in May 2008.[23] With North American Christians the country's leading source of tourists, 75,000 Canadians visited Israel in 2008.[24]

Israel's Tourist Office runs ads on Canadian Christian television that highlight "the spiritual dynamic that occurs during a trip to the Holy Land."[25] One ad says: "Visit Israel. You'll never be the same." Another tells the viewer, "Don't put your soul on hold."[26] Israel's marketing strategy included non-conventional advertising. Its Tourist Office came up with the idea for Bible and Roots Project, Peoples of the World Inscribe the Bible. According to its website, the goal is "to have, in the foothills of the Jerusalem mountains, a region of comprehensive Bible experience."[27] Prime Minister Stephen Harper inscribed the first Bible passage during the early 2007 Canadian launch of the Bible and Roots Project.[28]

Many Canadian ministries operate public tours of Israel. Back to the Bible Canada Tour of the Holy Land is one example. Founder of Canada's leading Christian talk show, David Mainse's Christian Ministries has also taken many pilgrims to Israel.[29]

A number of Christian organizations, many subsidized through tax write-offs, also work to send Jews to Israel. An international organization with a Canadian chapter, Bridges for Peace leads Project Ezra, which helps Jews in remote regions obtain passports, visas and other necessary goods for the trip to Israel.[30] Additionally, Bridges for Peace works with the Jewish Agency to pay for the "Exobus." A Christians for Israel (C4I) initiative, "the Exobus program ferries Jews from Eastern European villages to airports and seaports on the first leg of their journey to Israel."[31] Supported by a Canadian chapter, Holland-based C4I claims to have helped more than 80,000 Russian, Ethiopian and Indian Jews emigrate to Israel.[32]

In 1999 Rev. John Howson, director of Bridges for Peace, raised $68,000 (US) from his Winnipeg supporters for immigration initiatives.[33] His pitch: "God is calling the Jewish people back to the land of Israel for fulfillment of Bible prophecy and we should help them."[34] In 2005 McVety launched a campaign to raise a $1 million for an Israeli charity and immigration. "This is part of our 'Israel you're not alone campaign,'" McVety said.[35] The biggest source of Christian money for Israeli immigration comes from the John Hagee Ministries in Canada, which had raised more than $4 million in tax-deductible donations by early 2003.[36] According to a spokesperson, the Hagee Ministries regularly send cheques to Israeli groups.

While early Canadian Christian Zionism was spurred by British religious and imperial thinking, today's movement is heavily influenced by the social forces that support the U.S. empire. Some claim McVety and other Christian Zionists are funded by their U.S. counterparts.[37] They deny it. But there is no denying that Canada Christian College, for instance, "houses nearly two dozen [U.S.-based] evangelical tenants, including Oral Roberts Ministries, and ... John Hagee's Canadian command post," which sells up to $1 million a year worth of books and DVDs.[38]

Zionism is particularly strong among evangelical leaders who would like Canada to mimic socially regressive, God-fearing U.S. hyper capitalism. Less influential than their southern counterparts, about 10% of Canadians (three million) identify as evangelicals.[39]

An ardent supporter of U.S. imperialism, former head of the Alliance Party and International Trade Minister in Harper's cabinet, Stockwell Day has never drawn significant Jewish support. Understandably. In October 2004 Day said, "I will continue to speak and act in the House of Commons as if this is a Christian nation."[40] His Penticton British Columbia riding cannot have more than a handful of Jews yet Day has long backed Israel. An adviser to Day on international politics, Carleton University History Professor (emeritus) Paul Merkley says it's untrue that the "most important factor in keeping Israel secure is the [U.S.] Jewish vote" which is "less than two percent" of the total.[41] Rather, he said, it's evangelical Zionists who support Israel because "they sense that the people who hate Israel are the people who hate America. It's an adjunct of Conservative patriotism."[42] The President of the right wing Canadian Centre for Policy Studies, Joseph Ben-Ami, makes the same point about Canada. "The Jewish community in Canada is 380,000 strong; the evangelical community is 3.5 million. The real support base for Israel is Christians."[43]

Stockwell Day and Conservative MP James Lunney chair the Israel Allies Caucus. Formed in mid-2009 "amid a groundswell of Christian support for Israel around the world", a similar parliamentary lobby group was established in the U.S. Congress six months earlier.[44] The Israel Allies Caucus is an outgrowth of the Knesset's "Christian Allies Caucus." Josh Reinstein, director of the Knesset's Christian Allies Caucus, explains: "We hope that one day every parliament and government around the world will form a sister caucus to the Knesset's Christian Allies Caucus which will mobilize support for Israel around the world and promote Judeo-Christian values."[45]

Christian Zionists are often unabashed defenders of Israeli expansionism. Many of them believe Israel's present territory, including the West Bank and Golan Heights, represents a small fraction of the area God intends for a Jewish state.[46] John Hagee believes Israel has a right to be "10 times" its present size: from the Euphrates to the Nile.[47] Chairman of the board of Christians for Israel (International) and senior Pastor at New Covenant Christian Fellowship in Brantford Ontario, Dr. John Tweedie opposed Israel's disengagement from Gaza. "To see them [Israeli settlers] being pulled out and wrenched away from their homes is very disappointing."[48] In an interview with the *Hamilton Spectator* Tweedy argued that the Book of Joshua identifies Gaza as having been given to one of the 12 tribes of Israel.[49] "I have a Biblical worldview," explained Tweedy, "so I don't agree with trading land for peace."[50] In another speech Tweedie declared: "The pullout from southern Lebanon in 2000 did not prevent the second Lebanon war of 2006. The pullout from Gaza in 2005 did not stop Qassam rockets from being fired from Gaza onto Sderot and Ashkelon. Israel cannot pull out any more."[51]

Strongest in Canada, South Africa and the U.S., the International Christian Embassy Jerusalem (ICEJ) supports Zionist colonialism.[52] A board member of ICEJ, Stockwell Day's advisor Paul Merkley explains: "Palestinians aren't ready for a state for the time being, until they demonstrate an ability to govern themselves. Israel has no obligation to enter into discussions with them. I disagreed with Oslo; I thought it was mad. All Israel has to do is protect its population from them."[53]

Nomi Winkler, vice president of the hardline Toronto Zionist Council, gives high praise to Canadian Friends of ICEJ. "These people possess to an uncommon degree a quality which we have found sadly lacking in the [Jewish] community at large: their actions give life to their words! When we held demonstrations against the Toronto Star for its anti-Israel bias, they were with us; when we publicly protested Arab terrorism, they stood with us; when we demonstrated at the U.S. Consulate for Jonathan Pollard's freedom, they marched with us. ... when we asked various Jewish organizations to lend their names for letter of concern for the settlers' security, we were asked 'who else is signing?' Not [ICEJ's] Al Lazerte; he promptly faxed a letter — far stronger than ours — to the Prime Minister on behalf of the Canadian Friends of ICEJ. ... if ICEJ wishes to convert Jews to hasten the coming of the Messiah, let us produce an educational system, a religious and cultural milieu that will render our people impervious to their 'agenda and methodology.' In the meantime, for their generosity and actions on behalf of our people, I am beholden to Christian friends such as Canadian friends of ICEJ who came to Israel when the SCUDs were flying (and Jews rerouting to Florida) and who, God willing, will be joining our mission into Judea and Samaria [the West Bank] because they believe, as we do, that it is a sin to create an Arab terrorist state in eretz Israel."[54]

The new 'anti-Semitism'

The horrible history of anti-Semitism in Europe and elsewhere has, understandably, engendered support for a Jewish homeland. But, pro-Israel groups have manipulated this sympathy in an attempt to silence legitimate criticism of Israel.

While much less vicious than many European countries Canada does have an anti-Semitic legacy that needs to be acknowledged and countered. During the 1920s, 30s and 40s McGill University imposed restrictions on Jewish students.[55] At the same time Jews escaping Nazi persecution were refused entry into Canada. Unfortunately, the horrors of the Holocaust did not end institutionalized anti-Semitism. Many elite social clubs refused Jewish members into the 1960s while restrictive land covenants in some desirable neighbourhoods across the country made it impossible for Jews (and others) to buy property.

Thankfully Canada has changed significantly since "none is too many" was the order of the day in Ottawa. Christianity's decline combined with the rise of antiracist politics has significantly undercut anti-Semitism as a social force in Canada. Today, Jews are largely seen as "white" people. Canada's Jewish community is well represented among institutions of influence in this country and there is very little in terms of structural racism against Jews (which is not to say there isn't significant cultural stereotyping, which must be challenged). But in an inversion of reality, the more anti-Semitism declines as a social force the more it appears to concern the political elite.

A mere fig leaf of its formerly oppressive character, many Israeli apologists still cry anti-Semitism whenever it suits their cause. For Harper's Conservatives, for example, all opposition to Israeli policy was tantamount to anti-Semitism. In September 2009 Immigration Minister Jason Kenney compared a conflict between pro-and anti-Israel students at York University to Russian pogroms where hundreds, sometimes thousands of Jews were slaughtered. Kenney, a self-described "unapologetic supporter" of Israel, claimed: "Israel Apartheid Days on university campuses like York sometimes begin to resemble pogroms."[56] In April of that year Harper explained: "we are very concerned that, around the world, anti-Semitism is growing in volume and acceptance, justified … by opposition to Israel itself."[57] A month later Kenney denounced a "new anti-Semitism" that emanates from an alliance of Western leftists and Islamic extremists. In a statement bordering on Holocaust denial, Kenney said "the new anti-Semitism" is "even more dangerous than the old European anti-Semitism."[58] In a similar vein, Harper compared opposition parties' mild criticism of Israel to Hitlerism. In May 2008 Canwest reported: "some of the criticism brewing in Canada against the state of Israel, including from some members of Parliament, is similar to the attitude of Nazi Germany in the Second World War, Prime Minister Stephen Harper warned."[59]

Alongside its ardent support for Israel, the Harper government promoted the commemoration of Nazi crimes and the idea that anti-Semitism is worse than other forms of oppression. As this book went to print, Parliament appeared set to build a Holocaust museum, focusing on the suffering of Jews in Europe not indigenous people in Canada. Edmonton Conservative MP Tim Uppal, who introduced the private member's bill, explained: "After I had decided on [accepting Minister Peter Kent's proposal to put forward An Act to Establish a National Holocaust Monument], I ended up going to Israel with the Canada Israel committee in July. Being there, and learning what I did about the Holocaust and Israel, just made me feel more reassured that this was the right thing to do and get this bill passed."[60]

In mid-2009 the Conservatives created a National Task Force on Holocaust Research, Remembrance and Education. Headed by the fanatically pro-Israel group B'nai Brith, the Conservatives invested $1 million in the project.[61] This task force was tied to a similar European initiative. In the summer of 2007 Ottawa applied to join the Task Force for International Cooperation on Holocaust Education, Remembrance and Research, an organization that included 24 European nations and the U.S.. Created in 1998 the group promotes education of the genocide against European Jewry and "the unprecedented character of the Holocaust."[62] Ottawa was officially admitted to the club in mid-2009. "The admission of Canada into the International Holocaust Task Force represents the culmination of many years of dedication by this [Harper] government to furthering Holocaust education and remembrance in this country," said Frank Dimant, B'nai Brith Canada's executive vice-president. "Canadians can take pride in this wonderful achievement and know that Canada has now secured a position on the world stage as a leader in the field of Holocaust education and research."[63]

An outgrowth of the Holocaust Task Force, the first ever Interparliamentary Coalition to Combat anti-Semitism was held in February 2009 (Ottawa was set to host the second conference in October 2010). A number of conference participants expressed opposition to the growing worldwide boycott, divestment and sanctions (BDS) campaign. Minister Kenney, who led a 12-person Canadian delegation (the biggest), told the London conference: "The argument is with those whose premise is that Israel itself is an abomination and that the Jews alone have no right to a homeland. And in that sense anti-Zionism is anti-Semitism."[64] Kenney is unwilling to distinguish between a religion, a group of people living somewhere and a group that has displaced another group to build an ethno-theocratic state.

Associated with the Interparliamentary Coalition to Combat anti-Semitism the Canadian Parliamentary Coalition to Combat Anti-Semitism (CPCCA) has 21 MPs.[65] Begun in June 2009 the all party group launched an inquiry into Canadian anti-Semitism, what it describes as "this oldest and most enduring of hatreds."[66] In September 2009 CPCCA chair Anita Neville called on a pro-Israel audience to submit reports "because some of the submissions we've [CPCCA] been getting in the last couple of weeks aren't the kinds you or I would like to see."[67] Presumably, this Winnipeg MP was referring to submissions made by groups such as Independent Jewish Voices and others who reject the notion that opposing Israeli policy is tantamount to anti-Semitism.

During a July 2007 meeting of the Organization for Security and Co-operation in Europe (OSCE) Canada supported the appointment of a representative to the chair to report on anti-Semitism.[68] Despite calls for a change in OSCE policy, Ottawa supported recognizing prejudice against Jews as a unique phenomenon, not one among many forms of bigotry.[69] The OSCE meeting condemned all forms of racism, discrimination and "aggressive nationalism" but added: "Recognizing its unique and historic character, [we] condemn anti-Semitism without reservation, whether expressed in a traditional manner or through new forms and manifestations."[70]

The pro-Israel Jewish establishment lobbies for anti-Semitism to be prioritized over other forms of oppression despite the fact that Canada's Jewish community is relatively prosperous. In early 2002 the UN called on governments to examine "contemporary forms" of racism as they relate to "Africans and people of African descent, Arabs, Muslims and Jews."[71] The Canadian Jewish Congress was outraged. In a letter to the Liberal government they complained that not using the term anti-Semitism was "a retrograde step for it downplays the true nature of anti-Jewish animosity ... Merely condemning discrimination against 'Jews' does not reflect the historical phenomena of anti-Semitism as millennia-old hatred and persecution of the Jewish people. As the oldest and hardiest strain of the racism virus, anti-Semitism is on a quantitatively different plane from other examples cited."[72]

It is understandable that an institution created to promote one group does so, but does anyone believe Canadian Jews are subjected to the same amount of discrimination as Arabs, Muslims or Latin Americans, let alone Blacks or indigenous people in this country? The CJC's letter suggests a mindset bordering on the paranoid, or a willingness to disregard facts to get their way.

The Jewish establishment's campaign to prioritize the fight against anti-Semitism has been supported by many business leaders. In early 2007 the former head of the Bank of Montreal, Tony Comper, started Fighting Anti-Semitism Together (FAST), a coalition of non-Jewish business leaders and prominent individuals. Unfortunately, FAST is not an example of business leaders struggling for social justice. It is little more than a pro-Israeli front. The *Canadian Jewish News* reported: "Singling out Israel for blame in the Middle East conflict, even by those of good faith, is fanning anti-Semitism, Bank of Montreal president Tony Comper says. It may not be the intent, but the effect of condemning Israel alone is providing justification for hatred of Jews in Canada and internationally, Comper warned more than 400 business executives. ... In underscoring the serious threat of anti-Semitism worldwide, Comper suggested that 'a second Holocaust' is possible if Iran acquires nuclear arms and attacks Israel."[73] Comper added that CUPE Ontario's call to boycott Israel spurred anti-Semitism.[74]

FAST supporters included a who's who of the corporate elite: the former chairman of the Bank of Nova Scotia, Peter Godsoe; president and CEO of the Bank of Nova Scotia, Rick Waugh; CEO of Manulife Financial, Dominic D'Allessandro; chair of Bombardier, Laurent Beaudoin; president of Power Corporation, Andre Desmarais; president of the Yellow Pages Group, Marc Tellier; president of the National Bank, Real Raymond and others.[75]

For its part, B'nai Brith claimed its outreach in the business community, particularly its Award of Merit given to business executives, spurred the creation of FAST.[76] Whether B'nai Brith is as powerful as it claims is an open question. There is no doubt, however, that a big chunk of the business elite support B'nai Brith's pro-Israel advocacy. In 2000, for instance, a Power Corporation, Royal Bank and Bombardier sponsored evening at Montreal's Bonaventure Hilton Hotel raised $300,000 for the extremist pro-Israel group.[77]

In *The Holocaust Industry: Reflections on the Exploitation of Jewish Suffering*, Norman Finkelstein argues that the American Jewish establishment has exploited the memory of the Nazi Holocaust for financial and political gain and to further the interests of Israel. Finkelstein claims that discussion of the Nazi Holocaust grew exponentially after the June 1967 Six Day war. Prior to that war, which provided a decisive service to U.S. geopolitical aims in the Middle East, the genocide of European Jewry was a topic largely relegated to private forums and among left wing intellectuals.

Paralleling the U.S., the Nazi Holocaust was not widely discussed in Canada in the two decades after World War II. One study concluded that between 1945 and 1960 Canadian Jews exhibited "collective amnesia" regarding the six million Jews killed by the Nazis.[78] A professor of political studies at the University of Prince Edward Island, Henry Srebrnik, explains: "Before the 1967 Six Day War, Holocaust memorial commemorations were confined mostly to survivors themselves. I recall running across, by mere chance, Raul Hilberg's massive study The Destruction of the European Jews, in the McGill University library stacks, in 1966. It had been published, after much difficulty, in 1961, by a minor American press, after many others had rejected it.

"Amazing as it may seem to us today, the two major Jewish advocacy organizations working as one in the Jewish Community Relations Committee — B'nai Brith Canada and the Canadian Jewish Congress — displayed little interest [in discussing Nazi crimes] immediately after the war."[79]

When a National Jewish Black Book Committee (with Albert Einstein as honourary chair) published The Black Book: The Nazi Crime Against the Jewish People in 1946, "the book went almost unnoticed in Canada. Valia Hirsch, the executive secretary of the [National Jewish Black Book] committee, voiced her concerns that no meetings had been held in the Jewish communities of Montreal, Toronto, Ottawa, or Hamilton, to bring it to the attention of the Jewish community. The Canadian Jewish Congress had ordered 100 copies of the book in the summer of 1946, but had never bothered, according to Hirsch, to obtain them from Canada Customs. The CJC indicated a year later that they were no longer interested and 'cannot use them.'"[80]

Numerous commentators trace the established Jewish community's interest in Nazi crimes to the Six Day War. "The 1967 war," explained Professor Cyril Leavitt, "alarmed Canadian Jews. Increasingly, the Holocaust was invoked as a reminder of the need to support the Jewish state."[81] President of the Vancouver Jewish Community Center, Sam Rothstein concurred. "The 1967 war ... was the one development that led to a commitment by community organizations to become more involved in Holocaust commemoration. ... Stephen Cummings, the founder of the Montreal Holocaust Memorial Center, said that 'consciousness [of the Holocaust] has changed. Jews are much more proud, and that's a post-1967 [phenomenon]. It was the event that gave Jews around the world confidence.'"[82] Holocaust memorials proliferated after Israel smashed Egyptian-led pan-Arabism in six days of fighting, providing a decisive service to U.S. geopolitical aims. Nearly three decades after World War II, in 1972, the Canadian Jewish Congress and its local federations began to establish standing committees on the Nazi Holocaust.[83] The first Canadian Holocaust memorial was established in Montreal in 1977.

Nazi crimes, particularly Canada's various ties to these atrocities, should be widely studied and commemorated. The Nazi Holocaust, however, should not be used as ideological cover for Israeli crimes. That is an injustice to Palestinians and an insult to Hitler's victims.

Media

The media has played an important role in creating a pro-Israel political culture. This is largely a reflection of the fact that the dominant media is part of the ideological consensus generated by the economic and political elites, but there are also specific, "special" supporters of Israel. For example, the founder of Canada's largest media conglomerate (financially disintegrating in early 2010), Canwest Global, Izzy Asper helped establish the Canada-Israel Committee.[84] "I utterly supported [far right wing Prime Minister Menachem] Begin from the time I was 12 or 13," Asper explained. "Without him and his guerrilla revolt against the British, there would be no Israel."[85] In October 2002 Izzy claimed CNN, BBC, the *New York Times* and most of the rest of the English language media were biased against Israel.[86] "Too many of the journalists are lazy, or sloppy, or stupid," he explained. "They are ignorant of the history of the subject on which they are writing. Others are, plain and simple, biased, or anti-Semitic, or are taken captive by a simplistic ideology."[87] Leonard Asper, who took charge of Canwest in 1999, echoed his father's attack on the world media. "Racism is very difficult to prove, particularly when the accused do not openly state the reason for their attacks or their bias." He continued, "no reporter screams: 'I hate Jews.'"[88]

In August 2001 *Montreal Gazette* publisher Michael Goldblum suddenly resigned. After Goldblum quit, the *Globe and Mail* reported that "sources at the Gazette confirmed yesterday that senior editors at the paper were told earlier that month to run a strongly worded, pro-Israel editorial on a Saturday op-ed page."[89] The editorial, which was accompanied by a no rebuttal order from head office in Winnipeg, argued that Ottawa should back Israel's response to Palestinian suicide attacks, no matter how brutal.[90] The editorial explained: "Canada must recognize the incredible restraint shown by the Israeli government under the circumstances. … howsoever the Israeli government chooses to respond to this barbaric atrocity should have the unequivocal support of the Canadian government without the usual hand-wringing criticism about 'excessive force.' Nothing is excessive in the face of an enemy sworn to your anhilation."[91]

Rarely did Canwest publish opinions critical of Israel or sympathetic to Palestinians. The company's reporting was also heavily biased in Israel's favor. Unlike the *Globe and Mail* and *Toronto Star*, Canwest, which operates 11 major dailies, did not have a permanent correspondent in Israel. (Canwest did have a permanent correspondent at the UN, Stephen Edwards, who seemed to specialize in stories that promoted the idea the UN has an anti-Israel bias.) Instead, Canwest relied on wire services for its coverage of Palestine/Israel. This downplayed coverage of the region, which was usually to Israel's liking.

Relying on wire copy gave Canwest editors more flexibility on what to (or not to) publish. Still, sometimes this wire copy was deemed too evenhanded. Canwest papers repeatedly politicized Associated Press and Reuters dispatches from Israel/Palestine. A September 2004 Reuters article from Jerusalem referred to the Al-Aqsa Martyr Brigades but when *National Post* editors got hold of the copy they added the description "terrorist group."[92] The same month, reported the *New York Times*, "The [Ottawa] Citizen changed an A.P. dispatch to describe six of 10 Palestinians killed in the West Bank by Israeli troops as 'terrorists,' a description attributed to 'Palestinian medical officials.' The Associated Press had called those people 'fugitives.'"[93]

Canwest's reporting and commentary on Israel/Palestine was strongly biased in Israel's favor. But was it that much worse than the *Globe and Mail* or *Maclean's*? The CBC and *Toronto Star* may have appeared balanced compared to Canwest, but they still did a poor job of describing the conflict's power imbalance or the depth of Israeli belligerence. In 1995 the *Toronto Star* even boasted about a plaque commemorating a donation the paper made to Canada Park, which was built on illegally occupied land.[94]

Most Canadian media willing to seriously challenge Canadian support for Israeli policies are cash-strapped outfits unable to pay for regional correspondents.

The Israel lobby

In addition to friends like the bible literalists and sympathetic media operators, Israel has numerous organizations that lobby directly on its behalf. The Canada Israel Committee, Council for Israel and Jewish Advocacy, Israel Appeal Federations Canada and other pro-Israel lobbyists have long operated within a fortuitous political climate. They are pushing against an open door. What this means is best depicted contrasting it with lobbying when the door is closed. Imagine if a Canadian media operator, who owned a quarter of the country's private media, pushed his papers to run regular pro-North Korea articles. What would happen? The rest of the media would attack their competitor's Pro Kim Il Jong bias, advertisers would likely boycott the conglomerate and politicians might even consider a law restricting media ownership. Unlike Israel, the Canadian establishment is hostile to North Korea. Or what would happen to a group that promoted the Iranian regime? How many MPs would accept all expense paid trips to Iran if a pro-government group offered? Most MPs would shy away from the bad publicity.

These examples suggest that the effectiveness of lobbyists cannot be divorced from the prevailing political culture. Irving Abella, former president of the Canadian Jewish Congress, explained: "Domestic interest groups succeed only when the policies for which they are lobbying are those seen by the government as in the country's best interests."[95] Lobbyists can and do shape political decisions but it's usually within a narrow spectrum of options.

The Canada Israel Committee puts significant resources into sending members of Parliament to Israel. "Of all the free trips MPs accepted last year [2008], Israel outnumbered other destinations by nearly two to one ... According to Canada's ethics commissioner, the Canada-Israel Committee spent more than $200,000 to send 23 federal politicians and their spouses to the Middle East."[96] This is one reason why the all-party Canada-Israel Friendship Group, formed in 1981, included 43 members of Parliament.[97] Not surprisingly, CIC trips are designed to give a one-sided impression of Israel. In 1986 a Montreal Conservative MP complained that trip organizers did not let him talk to Palestinians living in West Bank refugee camps. "I just saw one side of the fence," Vincent Della Noce told the *Montreal Gazette*. "I was very disappointed that these guys [CIC] tried to brainwash me and abuse the little intelligence that I have."[98]

Federal politicians are not the only Canadians making the pilgrimage. Possibly as a way to thwart those who associate the plight of First Nations and Palestinians, pro-Israeli groups focus on Aboriginal leaders. In February 2006 the Canadian Jewish Congress (CJC) took Assembly of First Nations leaders, including Grand Chief Phil Fontaine, to Israel.[99] Two years later the CJC sponsored a delegation of First Nations women to the Golda Meir Mount Carmel International Training Centre.[100] For its part, B'nai Brith arranged a number of summer missions to Israel for First Nations clergy, educators and leaders.[101]

Concerned about growing Palestinian solidarity activism on campuses, pro-Israel groups targeted university administrators. The Canadian Council for Israel and Jewish Advocacy organized a week-long summer 2008 tour of Israel for the presidents of Ryerson, University of Waterloo, University of Toronto, University of Montreal, University of Saskatchewan, University of Ottawa, University of King's College and (for a day) McGill.[102] These trips were designed to solidify support for Israel. University of Toronto President David Naylor connected his visit to Israeli Apartheid Week (IAW). "This trip underscored something I've suspected for a while, namely, that Israeli Apartheid Week is ultimately irrelevant to the politics of the Middle East. The future of Israel and its neighbours will not be decided by a small group of activists who talk mostly to themselves on a few North American university campuses."[103]

A couple months after Naylor made these comments, the U of T sabotaged an IAW planning conference titled "Standing Against Apartheid: Building Cross-Campus Solidarity with Palestine." According to files uncovered through a Freedom of Information (FIPPA) request, U of T administrators decided to cancel the October 2008 room booking before it was even submitted. Executive Director of Hillel Toronto, Zac Kaye, informed the administration about the planned event, prompting a flurry of discussion between administrators, President Naylor included.[104] The FIPPA request generated more than 250 pages of documents containing references to Students against Israeli Apartheid, the U of T group organizing the event. Conference organizer Liisa Schofield summarized: "This is evidence of the unfettered access that the pro-Israel lobby has to the administrations at Canadian universities, and to the fact that the top administrators of Canadian universities are amenable to pressure from these groups."[105]

Administrators have become exceedingly hostile to Israeli Apartheid Week. In a flagrant affront to freedom of expression, McMaster banned use of the term "Israeli apartheid" during IAW 2008.[106] The next year, Carleton, Wilford Laurier and the University of Ottawa banned the IAW 2009 poster, which depicted an IDF helicopter shooting rockets at a child in Gaza holding a teddy bear.

Sponsored trips to Israel are not new even if they have become more regular and contentious. In 1994, 18 university presidents visited Israel with the CJC.[107] They met public officials (the foreign affairs and education ministers) and visited the occupied Golan Heights. York president Susan Mann explained: "This trip allowed us to renew the University's current agreements with the Hebrew University and the Jerusalem Centre for Public Affairs, and to develop stronger ties between York and Israeli institutions."[108]

Ties between Canadian and Israeli universities are often financed by pro-Israel donors. In 2008 the University of Manitoba began to send 40 students to Ben Gurion University each year.[109] The executive director of the U of M's Asper centre for Entrepreneurship, Robert Warren, said the partnership "is an expansion of the U of M and Tel-Aviv University exchange program that ran for three years. And it all began about five years ago when [pro-Israel power couple] Gerry [Schwartz] and Heather [Reisman] donated funds for a student exchange program between our school and one in Israel."[110]

Palestinian solidarity activism concerns university administrators partly because a number of the largest private donors to Canadian universities are staunch defenders of Israel. Supporters of the Palestinian cause make fewer donations to

Canadian universities and they are much less vocal about using their financial contributions to sway administrators. For their part, pro-Israel activists regularly call for donors to withhold their money to pressure universities into clamping down on Palestinian solidarity organizing.

When former Israeli PM Benjamin Netanyahu's September 2002 speech at Concordia was canceled due to protests, at least one major university donor backed out. Some board of governors members cited this as a rationale for a major clampdown on student rights. (See my book *Playing Left Wing* for more detail.) Marcel Dupuis, the university's director of corporate and foundation giving, conceded to the *Montreal Gazette* that "donors and alumni are saying 'if you don't get things in order, we're pulling the funding.'"[111] Later Concordia Rector Frederick Lowy further elaborated that there "have been repercussions already on fundraising."[112]

The Asper foundation sponsored Netanyahu's failed visit to Concordia. In a rant against the supposedly anti-Israel media a few weeks later, Izzy Asper, owner of Canada's largest media conglomerate, said: "We should withhold our financial support from those institutions [universities] that fail this obligation of educational integrity [to train reporters to support Israel]."[113] This was a threat that Asper could deliver on. In September 1999 he gave $2 million to the University of Manitoba, then the largest donation in the university's history, for an Asper Chair in International Business and Trade Law.[114] He also endowed the U of M's Asper centre for Entrepreneurship, a number of student scholarships and a national Holocaust and Human Rights studies program.[115]

Israeli-Canadian real estate magnate David Azrieli donated millions of dollars to Canadian universities. Two prominent buildings at Carleton are named in his honor while he established a fellowship at Concordia and a lecture series at McGill.[116] Azrieli, who fought in Ben Dunkelman's Seventh Brigade during the 1948 war, is a staunch Zionist. To commemorate the brutal Seventh

Brigade he paid for an amphitheatre to be built in the occupied Golan Heights.[117]

Mining magnate Seymour Schulich, probably the leading private donor to universities across the country, is also a strong supporter of Israel. Schulich claims to have made about $250 million in donations to universities, including a $20 million gift to Israel's Technion.[118] There is a Schulich School of Law at Dalhousie, Schulich School of Engineering at the University of Calgary, Schulich School of Medicine and Dentistry at the University of Western Ontario, Schulich School of Business at York as well as the Schulich Library of Science and Engineering and Schulich School of Music at McGill.

Sometimes donations buy direct Israel-focused academic work. Prominent pro-Israel family, the Bronfmans, provided more than $1.5 million to the University of Toronto in 1997 to create an Andrea and Charles Bronfman Chair in Israeli Studies, the first in the country.[119] "Fifty years after its rebirth, the miracle of modern Israel is of broad interest," said Charles Bronfman. "Andy and I are happy that students at the U of T will have the opportunity to delve into the social, political and economic revolutions that have taken place within this remarkable society."[120]

Endowing programs and departments buys political influence among administrators who busy themselves fundraising. Pro-Israel groups also fund student organizing. Concerned about growing Palestinian solidarity activism at York and Concordia, in 2003-2004 the United Jewish Appeal (Toronto) put up $1 million to fund pro-Israel activism at Canadian universities.[121] Part of this money was used to send 215 York students to Israel, "helping [them] better deal with anti-Israel agitation on campus."[122] Another portion of this funding was channeled through Betar Canada, which in one year spent $10,000 to $15,000 on pro-Israel pamphlets and speakers at York.[123] Additionally, Betar helped enlist pro-bono lawyers to fight fines York levied against pro-Israeli students.

In August 2009 activists from across North America converged on Concordia for a conference titled Israel on Campus: Defending Our Universities. Concordia President Judith Woodsworth spoke at the event designed: "1. to bring a powerful analytic focus to bear on the mounting threat to academic freedom and free inquiry represented by the growth of antisemitism, masquerading as anti-Zionism and anti-Israelism, on our campuses, and 2. to develop, on the basis of a clear set of informing principles, a 'Campus Defense Council' tasked with an ongoing, coordinated, and persistent international campaign to 'take back the campus'."

The power of empire

Canada gains little from Israel's occupation, which costs Palestinians so dearly. Despite limited direct benefits Ottawa goes along with Israeli policy in the West Bank, Gaza and Golan Heights. Because the direct economic benefits are limited many have concluded that the Jewish lobby described above is responsible for Canada's position. This is exaggerated.

Other major Canadian foreign-policy decisions may provide perspective. From the troops that joined the British in Sudan in 1885 to the thousands of soldiers who pillaged and murdered the Boers during the war of 1898-1902 in South Africa, Canada has long sided with empire. Precipitating the Cold War, Canada sent 4,000 troops to halt the Russian Revolution and then sided with the fascists in 1936, blocking weapons and volunteers from joining the army of Spain's elected government, all the while arming the Japanese as they occupied Korea and massacred the Chinese. In the first major UN military operation, Canada sent 27,000 troops between 1950-53 to fight in Korea — largely as part of the U.S. campaign against nationalism and communism in East Asia.

Half a century later, 18 Canadian fighter jets dropped 530 bombs in 682 sorties during NATO's 78-day illegal bombing campaign of Serbia. Justified as a great humanitarian endeavour the spring 1999 campaign was designed to weaken Russia, reaffirm NATO and push "free" market economics.

Not long after bombing Serbia, thousands of Canadians fought a counterinsurgency war in Afghanistan. A handful of Canadian corporations benefitted from reconstruction projects in Afghanistan and some embraced the mission to justify an expansion of the army, but the occupation was largely about supporting the Washington-led West's geostrategic position vis-a-vis Russia, China and Iran.

How much direct economic benefit did Canada derive from helping to overthrow Haiti's elected government in 2004? Some sweatshop and mining interests profited from Canadian policy, but most of the benefits were indirect. Alongside Washington and Paris, Ottawa participated in the coup because Jean Bertrand Aristide's government was an obstacle to the full implementation of the "free" market agenda. By increasing the minimum wage and refusing to privatize a handful of state owned companies Aristide disturbed Canadian powerbrokers' vision of Haiti as the hemisphere's preeminent reserve of cheap labor. To a large extent, officials in Ottawa helped overthrow Aristide because they could. Few powerful people were concerned about this predominantly black country and so there was little political cost in ousting the elected government. While the social costs for most Haitians were significant it was of only limited international or domestic political consequence.

Palestinian rights garner much more international attention than those of Haitians. Still, there isn't any significant source of power in Canada backing Palestinians so the point is largely the same. Social justice, humanism and morality rarely motivate Canadian foreign policy. Instead, power is what drives foreign affairs and Palestinians have never had much of it. Long under Ottoman rule, then British control after World War I, the Palestinians were an oppressed and relatively powerless people. Palestinians also had the misfortune of living on land claimed by a predominantly European political movement.

While few cared about the indigenous population, the pre-state Zionist movement was supported by influential political currents within Europe and North America. For decades the British saw Zionism as a beachhead to strengthen their control over the Suez Canal and the main trade route to India. Since its founding, particularly after 1967, U.S. strategists have considered Israel an important ally in the heart of the (oil-producing) Middle East. An internal 1958 U.S. National Security Council memorandum, for instance, argued that a "logical corollary" of opposition to radical Arab nationalism "would be to support Israel as the only strong pro-West power left in the near East."[124]

In the late 1950s and 60s Washington was wary about the increasing popularity of Egyptian-led Arab nationalism. Secular pan-Arabism threatened the kingdoms in the Gulf oil-producing countries and Washington was concerned about the stability of Saudi Arabia's monarchy.[125] For many years Israel acted as a barrier to the pressure Nasser's Egypt placed on the Gulf oil-producing states and ultimately the IDF smashed pan-Arabism in the 1967 war.

Washington was ecstatic. By undermining the region's decrepit monarchies, pushing nationalist economic reforms and potentially strengthening the region's ability to resist foreign dominance, successful Arab nationalism threatened U.S. control over Middle Eastern oil. Israel was hostile to pan-Arabism for similar reasons. It depended on a weak and divided Arab world to maintain its Jewish/white supremacy, belligerence in the region and expansionism. The Washington/Tel Aviv axis was largely based on these shared geostrategic interests, which Ottawa supported.

Canadian policy towards the Middle East has largely been designed to enable U.S. imperial designs on a strategic part of the planet. The region's geopolitical importance to Washington — combined with limited Canadian business activity in the region — means that Canadian policymakers are largely focused on the interests of our southern neighbour. Noam Chomsky has commented that U.S. policy in the region — from its invasion of Iraq to its unflinching support of Israel — is largely motivated by a desire to control the region's "stupendous energy reserves." To continue the logic it would be fair to say that Canadian policy towards the Middle East is designed, above all else, to guarantee the U.S.-led West's control over the region's energy resources.

Support for Israel has largely mirrored different governments' relationships to Washington. The federal governments most enthralled with Washington have been Israel's biggest cheerleaders. The Harper and Brian Mulroney governments were staunchly pro-Israel and U.S.. Conversely, the two least "Israel no matter what it does" governments in Canadian history were led by Pierre Trudeau and Jean Chretien. Trudeau and Chretien were also the least "U.S. right or wrong" administrations since John Diefenbaker (who came to power partly by criticizing the Liberal government for siding with Washington instead of London during Israel's 1956 invasion of Egypt).

Pre-state Canadian support for Zionism was tied to British imperial designs. Prime Minister Mackenzie King, for instance, ardently defended British imperialism, which is why he openly supported Zionism for decades. In the 1940s Britain backed away from its pro-Zionism stance and so King equivocated on his earlier position.

Commentators often claim pro-Israeli policy is motivated by a search for Jewish votes. The numbers don't add up. Just over one percent of the population in the 2006 census, 315,120 Canadians, identified their origin as Jewish, either alone or in combination with another ethnicity (the actual number of Jews is slightly higher but religion is counted every other census).[126] Jews were the 25th largest group defined by ethnic origin and only a handful of electoral ridings have a significant concentration of Jews.[127] It's true that Jews have high levels of political engagement, are well represented in positions of influence and are a relatively prosperous minority group.[128] But this is a relatively new phenomenon and should not be exaggerated. Additionally, voting patterns suggest few Canadian Jews vote based on Ottawa's policy towards Israel.

There is an inverse correlation between pro-Israel governments and Jewish support. Trudeau and Chretien, for instance, garnered more support from the Jewish community than either Harper or Mulroney.[129] Repeatedly reelected in Montreal's Mount Royal, which was almost 50% Jewish in the mid-1960s, Trudeau distanced Ottawa from Israeli conduct more than any other Prime Minister before him.[130] (Trudeau also appointed the first Jew to the federal cabinet, Herb Gray, while Jack Austin, Barney Danson and Robert Kaplan served in subsequent Trudeau cabinets.) At the same time, Trudeau gradually moved Ottawa away from Washington's Middle East policy. "From 1967 to 1972, Canada voted with the United States on 81% of all Middle East resolutions, 44% of the time with the countries of the European economic community, and it maintained 'company' with Israel on 44% of all votes."[131] As the Trudeau government got its bearings this pattern was reversed. From 1973 to 1977 Ottawa voted with the Europeans on 89% of Middle East resolutions and with Washington 38% of the time (and maintained company with Israel 28% of the time).[132] As part of building a more independent-minded foreign-policy Trudeau moved Canada away from Lester Pearson inspired liberal internationalism, which largely advanced American designs in the Middle East. According to Trudeau, liberal internationalism did not necessarily reflect Canadian business interests. He wanted a tighter linkage between the costs and benefits associated with international endeavours.[133]

Trudeau's governments opened seven new missions in Arab capitals and by prioritizing Canadian business interests in the Middle East, Trudeau effectively downgraded Israel's importance.[134] Moves to bring Canada closer to the Arab world were rooted in a broader economic nationalism and spurred by Arab countries' willingness to use their growing economic might. During the October 1973 (Yom Kippur) war a number of Arab countries launched an oil boycott of Western countries supporting Israel. After 1975 about 15% of Canadian oil came from the Middle East and a leaked 1976 cabinet memo concluded that a disruption of imports would have "serious effects" on Canada's economy, causing "oil shortages and unemployment."[135] Ultimately, the boycott was not vigorously pursued and had only limited impact on Canadian political and economic relations in the Arab world.[136] Still, it provided a counterweight to the pro-Israel pull of U.S. imperialism.

The most direct example of economic interests influencing relations with Israel took place in 1979. Short-lived Conservative Prime Minister Joe Clark announced plans to relocate the embassy from Tel Aviv to Jerusalem, effectively recognizing Israeli sovereignty over the city. Arab threats of economic sanction pushed the CEOs of Bell Canada, Royal Bank, ATCO and Bombardier, which all had important contracts in the region, to lobby Clark against making the move. An embarrassed federal government backtracked.[137]

Even though Canadian support for Israel is mainly motivated by geopolitics, not direct business interests, Ottawa has worked diligently to expand economic ties with Israel (through a trade agreement and industrial research most notably). More than ever Canadian and Israeli high tech companies are interdependent and there is growing trade between the two countries. Still, Israel is a long way away and only has seven million inhabitants. From the perspective of Canadian capitalism, the Arab world has more workers and resources to exploit, as well as markets to sell to.

In practice it has rarely been an either-or proposition. Canadian corporate interests in the Middle East have flourished alongside Ottawa's support for an aggressive Israel. The foreign-policy establishment has long understood that Israel is a valuable Western asset. An internal report circulated at External Affairs during the 1947 UN negotiations to create Israel summarized Ottawa's thinking: "The plan of partition gives to the western powers the opportunity to establish an independent, progressive Jewish state in the Eastern Mediterranean with close economic and cultural ties with the West generally and in particular with the United States."[138]

External Affairs Minister Lester Pearson repeated this thinking in a 1952 memo to cabinet. "With the whole Arab world in a state of internal unrest and in the grip of mounting anti-western hysteria, Israel is beginning to emerge as the only stable element in the whole Middle East area."[139] Pearson went on to explain how "Israel may assume an important role in Western defence as the southern pivot of current plans for the defence" of the Eastern Mediterranean.[140]

On occasion public officials have openly touted Israel's value to Western imperialism. In a February 1956 speech to the House of Commons Liberal MP Don Carrick said: "Israel could be an outpost and source of security for the Western world in the Middle East ... [now that] the Egyptians have driven the British out of the Suez ... Israel could constitute an arsenal for the democracies of the free world in the Middle East."[141] External Affairs Minister Don Jamieson echoed this sentiment in an October 1977 speech. "Israel is an increasingly valuable ally of the West and Jews and non-Jews alike should see to it that Israel remains ... an ally of the Western world. ... We in Canada must see to it that when Israel is making such tremendous sacrifices, we should stand ready to help Israel with oil and material assistance."[142]

In the autumn of 1986 Canada Israel Committee national chairman Sidney J. Spivak added: "It [Israel] represents a secure bastion for Western interests in a most troubled and unstable region."[143] More recently, Minister Jason Kenney described attacks against Israel as a threat to Canada's interests. "The existential threat faced by Israel on a daily basis is ultimately a threat to the broader Western civilization. ... Israel [is abused] as a kind of representative of the broader West."[144]

How long Israel will continue in this geostrategic role for the U.S. empire is unknown, but so long as it does, there will be a powerful force pushing Canada to be one-sidedly pro-Israel.

Chapter 10
Changing course

Many Canadians may be satisfied with their country's foreign policy towards Israel as outlined above. Others — I suspect a significant majority — when confronted with the facts, will be troubled, upset and even angry about what is being done in their name. In fact, despite Ottawa's strident support for Israel, grassroots opposition to that country's policies has never been greater. During Israel's December 2008/January 2009 assault on Gaza Canadians displayed an unprecedented level of solidarity. Demanding Israeli crimes not be committed in their name, eight Jewish women were arrested at Toronto's Israeli consulate two weeks into the attack. The next day two dozen Montrealers shut down the city's Israeli consulate for a few hours. Later that week four London, Ont. activists directed their ire against a local politician by occupying the office of Conservative MP Ed Holder. They called on the Harper government to reverse course and condemn Israel's assault. To draw attention to the province's recently signed trade agreement with Israel six Montrealers locked themselves together in the office of Quebec's Economic and Development Minister. The protesters also called for Premier Jean Charest to heed public opinion and pronounce himself against the destruction of Gaza.

In response to Israel's offensive Montreal held probably the largest pro-Palestinian demonstration in Canadian history. Between 12,000 and 17,000 (possibly as many as 25,000) people marched on January 10, 2009. "Jews, Christians, Muslims, anglos, francos, grandmothers and children walked together yesterday in the bitter cold to call for an immediate ceasefire in [Gaza]," noted the Montreal Gazette.[1] The march was endorsed and organized by all three major Quebec union federations and most of the province's social groups. The same day thousands marched in Montreal against the destruction of Gaza there were 18 demontrations across the country, many of them with as many as 1,000 people, even in smaller cities like Hamilton and Edmonton. Throughout Israel's assault there were only a handful of indoor events supporting Israel.

Despite the political/media establishment's pro-Israel stance, most Canadians do not view Israel favourably. A few weeks after the Gaza onslaught the *Globe and Mail* cited a poll that found that 52% of Canadians believe Israel plays a negative role in the world. Only 28% of respondents thought it played a positive role (other polls show similar results).[2] These numbers bode well for people who organize against Canada's support for Israeli belligerence and in favor of Palestinian rights. So do surveys commissioned by pro-Israel groups that suggest the more Canadians know about the conflict the greater their sympathy for Palestinians.[3]

Educating Canadians about what is being done in their name is the key to changing our foreign policy. Only when Canadians understand the reality of Israel, when they learn that their government takes the side of Israel despite its glaring human rights violations, will change be possible. The work ahead mostly consists of talking to the uninvolved, handing out leaflets, putting up posters and organizing talks. But sometimes it may be necessary to yell at Israeli apologists or barricade offices. We need to create a political climate where justifying killing Palestinians and stealing their land is no longer acceptable.

If people are prepared to suffer the legal consequences it would be useful to peacefully disrupt press conferences and speeches by prominent pro-Israeli cabinet ministers such as Jason Kenney. Canadian politicians cannot be allowed to justify horrendous crimes without being called on it. Their justifications for Israeli crimes need to be firmly and directly denounced. When picketing or disrupting meetings in the Jewish community, ideally actions would be led by anti-Zionist Jews. If possible, we should respect sensibilities regarding anti-Semitism, but at the same time there is no need to pander to manufactured fears.

Whenever possible, actions should be creative. When a group of us interrupted a 60th anniversary speech by the Israeli ambassador in April 2008 we threw political confetti. The multicoloured pieces of paper passed a message about Palestinian dispossession and contributed to the action's chaotic effect. For the protesters the confetti added a lighthearted element. Disrupting the ambassador's speech forced the media present to cover opposition to Israeli policy, which they likely would not have done otherwise. Judging by the event organizers' reaction it was a success. Not used to being confronted, a number of the most prominent pro-Israel activists in Montreal freaked out.

Of course, pro-Israel groups are worried about declining support, which is why they constantly shout "anti-Semitism". There are now dozens of Palestinian solidarity groups across the country and Canadian social movements have never been more critical of Israel. (See the Resources section of the book for a list of groups)

Toronto is a particularly important battleground for both pro-and anti-Israel lobbying. To shore up its image in the city, the Israeli consulate launched a wide-ranging "Brand Israel" campaign in 2008/09. A test case for an international "Brand Israel" launch, pro-Israel advertising was put up across Toronto. Even though Canada already had the largest number of Israeli diplomats per capita in late 2009 Israel added a deputy consul in Toronto and a staff member to the embassy.[4]

Adding the deputy consul "reflects the importance of ... [Toronto]," consular Amir Gissin explained, "as an arena for Israel from a PR, cultural and commercial point of view."[5] According to the *Canadian Jewish News*, one reason Israel added to its Toronto consulate was Israeli Apartheid Week (IAW).[6] Begun in Toronto, IAW has gone global. Israeli apologists are not happy. As IAW 2009 ended B'nai Brith took out a full page advertisement in the *National Post* calling on university administrators to shut down the 2010 version.

Pro-Israel commentators claim IAW and grassroots criticism of Israel, more generally, is somehow "anti-Semitic." They are wrong, of course. But, it is true that Palestinian suffering receives more attention than other world atrocities (such as the millions killed in Eastern Congo or the thousands killed in the aftermath of the Canadian backed coup in Haiti). The point of our protests must not just be Palestinian suffering but rather Canadian complicity with that suffering. That complicity is what should compel Canadians to focus on what is happening in Israel. By not focusing on Canada's responsibility for the conflict Palestinian solidarity activists have opened themselves up to attacks regarding their single-minded devotion to Israel's crimes. To undercut this self-serving argument, which is often an insinuation of anti-Semitism, it is important to make our critique of Canadian foreign-policy more explicit. The multiple forms of aid this country provides Israel, and that country's dependence on foreign support, make it important to devote significant political energy to weakening Canada's support for Israeli belligerence. Palestine is not Tibet. Canadian responsibility for Chinese colonialism in Tibet does not compare with our responsibility for Palestinian dispossession.

Focusing primarily on American support for Israel, or that country's actions divorced from its international patrons, are other ways of shirking our responsibility. As Canadians we have responsibility for what our government and other institutions do in our name. How Canadian public and, to a lesser extent, private institutions undermine Palestinian self-determination should be our primary concern. "We live in Canada," notes Independent Jewish Voices co-president Sid Sniad, "Canada is the only place where we can hope to shift the balance of political forces. And shifting the political forces here is the only practical leverage we have to exert influence over what happens in Palestine. So it is the people in Canada whom we must mobilize to compel change in Canadian state policies and practices."[7] Simply put, the best way to improve the prospects for Palestinian liberation is to get this country's foreign affairs house in order.

Anger with Israeli conduct should be channeled to where it can be most politically useful. Usually the best way to do that is to target complicit Canadian institutions. There is also a need for long-term popular education and organizing, not simply opposition to specific Israeli actions.

The boycott divestment sanctions (BDS) campaign is an initiative that can spur long-term organizing efforts. Launched in July 2005 by 171 Palestinian unions, associations and civil society organizations, it states that "non-violent punitive measures should be maintained until Israel meets its obligation to recognize the Palestinian people's inalienable right to self-determination and fully complies with the precepts of international law by:

"1. Ending its occupation and colonization of all Arab lands and dismantling the Wall;

"2. Recognizing the fundamental rights of the Arab-Palestinian citizens of Israel to full equality; and

"3. Respecting, protecting and promoting the rights of Palestinian refugees to return to their homes and properties as stipulated in UN resolution 194."[8]

Rather than deal with the issues raised by the boycott and disinvestament campaign the corporate media has vilified BDS campaigners. CUPE-Ontario was repeatedly condemned for passing a resolution in support of BDS and the United Church was called anti-Semitic for even considering the Palestinian groups' requests. This should be expected. The Canadian media largely opposed the boycott of South Africa even though Canada was less complicit with that form of apartheid than the current Israeli version. (Canada did have greater public and private ties to apartheid South Africa than is commonly understood. See *Black Book of Canadian Foreign Policy* or *Ambiguous Champion* for details). More than two decades after the Sharpeville massacre and six years after Soweto exploded, the *Globe and Mail* argued that "disinvestment would be unwittingly an ally of apartheid" since Canadian investments brought progressive ideas.[9]

South African boycott campaigners organized for years before they won any major victories. The obstacles will be bigger with Israel. Already, however, the BDS campaign has made some strides, particularly in Europe and South Africa. Students at Sussex University voted in a referendum to boycott Israeli goods while Britain's six million-member Trade Union Congress, the Irish Congress of Trade Unions and South Africa's COSATU union federation all passed resolutions supporting BDS.[10] In February 2009 South African dockworkers refused to unload an Israeli ZIM Lines ship and "Norway's $400 billion-plus wealth fund has excluded Israeli company Elbit Systems for supplying surveillance equipment for the separation barrier in the West Bank," Reuters reported in September 2009.[11] And that same month, "The U.S. pension fund giant, TIAA-CREF... divested from Africa Israel Investments, owned by Israeli billionaire Lev Leviev [who is heavily invested in the West Bank] ... The statements came in response to a letter initiated by a pro-Palestinian group, Adalah-NY."[12]

Many Canadian social groups such as Independent Jewish Voices and Quebec's most active student federation, ASSE, have joined the BDS movement. So has Quebec Solidaire, a new left-wing party with one member in the National Assembly. A number of unions, including the Canadian Union of Postal Workers, CUPE-Ontario and the Teachers Federation in Quebec have also joined BDS campaigners.

As an educational tool the BDS campaign can advance the Palestinian cause in Canada. Some narrow successes could be expected in the short run, especially regarding Canadian ties to illegal settlements. But, many Canadian institutions are deeply committed to and integrated with Israel, which makes it unrealistic to expect anything approaching a widespread boycott of Israel in the short or medium term. Over the longer term a vibrant BDS campaign could vastly reduce Canadian ties to Israel. That will probably not happen, however, since Israel is highly dependent on North American financial, military, ideological and diplomatic support. If Canada, together with Israel's other major allies, were about to impose economic sanctions (as Canada did against South Africa in 1986) Israel would almost certainly make the necessary concessions to the Palestinians.

What long-term campaigns should the Canadian solidarity movement focus on?

Halt all weapons sales to Israel, which is among the world's most conflict prone countries. This campaign has natural allies among peace and disarmament groups.

Revoke the Jewish National Fund's charitable status. Public money should not support a racist institution active in the Occupied Territories. Do most Canadians want millions of their tax dollars supporting JNF racism? The problem is that very few people are familiar with the matter. That could change with the launching of a nationwide campaign: "No public money for Jewish National Fund racism." People could start by putting up hundreds of thousands of stickers or posters on the issue and asking social groups to sign on to a statement asking the federal government to rescind the JNF's charitable status. JNF fundraising galas are held regularly across the country. People could leaflet, chant and peacefully disrupt these dinners, particularly when public officials participate. The JNF is at the heart of Israeli apartheid and drawing attention to this institution is a way to discuss the racism intrinsic to Zionism. Even if Revenue Canada failed to act against the JNF — among the most politically connected pro-Israel charities — our tax collection agency needs to be pressured into canceling the charitable status of other groups funding West Bank settlers or lobbying on Israel's behalf.

Rescind security agreements with Israel and CSIS/Mossad ties.

Unions should be pressured to get rid of their State of Israel Bonds.

Boycott Indigo/Chapters/Coles bookstores. The company's majority shareholders Heather Reisman and Gerry Schwartz must suffer a financial penalty for funding Israeli mercenaries. As the most flagrant example of private Canadian financing for Israeli militarism, the ongoing Indigo campaign tests the BDS movement's capacity to effect change. Additionally, the campaign has natural allies among independent bookstores, which have been decimated by the chain's monopolistic activities.

Outside of specific BDS campaigns we should direct anger towards public institutions or officials. We want to "de-ethnicize" the conflict. This is not an Arab or Jewish issue but rather one of global importance about basic human dignity. The antiracist sectors of Canada's Jewish community have made major strides in recent years. Groups such as Independent Jewish Voices, Not In Our Name, Jewish Voices for Peace, the International Jewish Anti-Zionist Network, Women in Solidarity with Palestine and Jews for a Just Peace, have undercut the notion that all Canadian Jews support Israeli policy or Zionism. But these groups are unlikely to become dominant voices within the Jewish community until there is a shift in Canada's political culture. It's time to "de-zionize" our political culture, which is a struggle that must engage Canadians of all backgrounds.

Support for Israel can be viewed in isolation but it should not be completely divorced from a wider foreign-policy discussion. The Palestinian solidarity movement will thrive as part of the struggle to shift Canadian foreign policy away from slavish support for empire. The Harper government's sabre rattling towards Iran, for instance, is spurred by support for Israel, which is part of a broader pro-U.S. empire orientation.

In place of the foreign-policy establishment's pro-empire orientation there is a need to articulate an independent-minded policy rooted in social justice. My *Black Book of Canadian Foreign Policy* concludes with a number of proposals: reduce the military budget, pull Canada out of NATO, use aid to support elected governments etc. One proposal to add to that list is a push for legislation committing Ottawa to uphold the Charter of Rights and Freedoms in foreign affairs. Canadians support the Charter and a broad cross-section of groups working on foreign policy issues could support this demand. As part of this campaign Palestine solidarity groups could launch a constitutional challenge directed at Canadian support for Israel. Our courts should be asked to rule that Ottawa's policies towards Palestine contravene the Charter of Rights and Freedoms.

On a broader level it is essential to democratize Canadian foreign-policy. More than other aspects of government policy, foreign affairs is dominated by a small elite. Most of the population is simply shut out of the discussion and until that changes the interests of the foreign policy establishment will take precedence over social justice. As always the first step is to educate ourselves so that we can educate others.

Notes

Introduction

1 Israeli Apartheid, 4
2 Palestine, 215
3 Israeli Apartheid, 4
4 Apartheid Israel, 48
5 Apartheid Israel, 48
6 Israeli Apartheid, 33
7 Israeli Apartheid, 126
8 http://www.fmep.org/analysis/analysis/israeli-attempt-to-impose-absentee-property-law-to-arab-property-in-east-jerusalem
9 Israeli Apartheid, 49
10 http://en.wikipedia.org/wiki/Arab_citizens_of_Israel
11 http://www.counterpunch.org/neumann10142009.html
12 Israeli Apartheid, 53
13 http://electronicintifada.net/v2/article10701.shtml
14 Electronic Intifada Nov 30 2009
15 http://news.bbc.co.uk/2/hi/7692983.stm
16 Defending the Holy Land, 5
17 Defending the Holy Land, 231
18 Defending the Holy Land, 35

Chapter 1

1 Evangelics and Israel, 16
2 Non-Jewish Zionism, 24
3 Non-Jewish Zionism, 25
4 Non-Jewish Zionism, 63
5 Non-Jewish Zionism, 63
6 For the Time is at Hand, 9
7 http://www.biographi.ca/009004-119.01-e.php?&id_nbr=6307
8 Canada and Palestine, 10
9 A Coat of Many Colors, 149
10 http://en.wikipedia.org/wiki/Henry_Wentworth_Monk
11 Righteous Victims, 42 & http://en.wikipedia.org/wiki/Henry_Wentworth_Monk
12 Canadian Jewish News Apr 10 2008
13 Canadian Jewish News Apr 10 2008
14 Canada and Palestine, 10
15 Canada and Palestine, 10
16 For the Time is at Hand, 9
17 http://christianactionforisrael.org/isreport/cdn-isr.html

18 A Coat of Many Colors, 149
19 Allies for Armageddon, 80 & Christian Zionism, 32
20 From Immigration to Integration, 124
21 http://www.christianzionism.org/Article/Wagner06.asp
22 Taking Root, 182
23 A Coat of Many Colors, 149
24 Canada and Palestine, 80
25 From Immigration to Integration, 126
26 Canada and Palestine, 34
27 Canada and the Birth of Israel, 13
28 Canada and the Birth of Israel, 13
29 From Immigration to Integration, 126
30 Lillian and Archie Freeman, 255
31 Non-Jewish Zionism, 70
32 Canada and Palestine, 13
33 Righteous Victims, 41
34 Righteous Victims, 63
35 Righteous Victims, 33
36 Le Mouvement Juif au Canada, 244 & Taking Root, 194
37 Jews and French Quebeckers, 49
38 Jews of Windsor, 75
39 The End of the Peace Process, 216
40 One Palestine, Complete
41 Canada and Palestine, 42
42 Canada and Palestine, 41
43 A Coat of Many Colors, 166
44 Taking Root, XXIV
45 Canada and Palestine, 41
46 Rabbi Dr. Herman Abramowitz, 69
47 Canada's Jews, 178
48 A Coat of Many Colors, 156
49 A Coat of Many Colors, 156
50 From Immigration to Integration, 130
51 Taking Root, 200
52 Non-Jewish Zionism, 193
53 Louis Fitch Q. C., 23
54 An Olive Branch on the Family Tree, 89
55 An Olive Branch on the Family Tree, 89
56 Western Imperialism in the Middle East 1914-1958, 148
57 Taking Root, 182
58 Canada's Jews, 343
59 From Immigration to Integration, 132
60 Fabled City, 151

61 Domestic Battleground, 40
62 Taking Root, 198
63 Fabled City, 151
64 Canada and Palestine, 100
65 Canada's Jews, 342
66 ZNet May 6 2008
67 ZNet May 6 2008 & From Immigration to Integration, 132 & Taking Root, 192
68 http://www.zmag.org/znet/viewArticle/17552
69 All That Remains, 564
70 ZNet May 6 2008
71 Israeli Apartheid, 1
72 Israeli Apartheid, 15 & The Iron Cage, 120
73 The Iron Cage, 120
74 From Immigration to Integration 127
75 Canada and Palestine 100

Chapter 2

1 Personal Policy Making, 3
2 Canada and the Birth of Israel, 70
3 Canada and the Birth of Israel, 72
4 Canadian Maverick, 230
5 The Making of the Arab-Israeli Conflict, 18
6 Canada and the Birth of Israel, 60 & Personal Policy Making, 5
7 http://www.jewishvirtuallibrary.org/jsource/myths/canada.html#_edn11
8 The Making of the Arab-Israeli Conflict, 29
9 http://christianactionforisrael.org/un/unscop2.html
10 http://christianactionforisrael.org/un/unscop3.html
11 The Fall and Rise of Israel, 381
12 Le Canada et le conflit Israelo-Arab, 30
13 Canadian-Arab Relations, 10 & Domestic Battleground, 127
14 Personal Policy Making, 18
15 Canadian Maverick, 247
16 Personal Policy Making, 24
17 Personal Policy Making, 24
18 Personal Policy Making, 19
19 Personal Policy Making, 26
20 Personal Policy Making, 72
21 Personal Policy Making, 72
22 http://palestine-studies.org/enakba/diplomacy/Khalidi,%20Revisiting%20the%201947%20UN%20Partition%20Resolution.pdf.
23 ZNet May 6 2008
24 http://www.palestine-studies.org/enakba/diplomacy/Khalidi,%20Revisiting%20the%201947%20UN%20Partition%20Resolution.pdf
25 Canada and Palestine, 134
26 Domestic Battleground, 129
27 Domestic Battleground, 136
28 Personal Policy Making, 78 & 82
29 Personal Policy Making, 86
30 Halifax Chronicle-Herald Nov 20 2001 & Canada and the Middle East, 10
31 http://www.canpalnet-ottawa.org/Canada-Israel.html
32 Personal Policy Making, 81
33 Canadian-Arab Relations, 62
34 Canada and the Birth of Israel, 117
35 Ethnic Cleansing of Palestine, 29
36 Ethnic Cleansing of Palestine, 18
37 Ethnic Cleansing of Palestine, 34
38 Personal Policy Making, 73
39 Personal Policy Making, 73 & Domestic Battleground, 129
40 Personal Policy Making, 94
41 Personal Policy Making, 91
42 The Rise and Fall of a Middle Power, 79
43 Canada and the Birth of Israel, 129
44 Canada and the Birth of Israel, 135
45 Canada and Palestine, 123
46 Fabled City, 149
47 http://www.zmag.org/znet/viewArticle/17554
48 http://www.winchevskycentre.org/institutions/noneistoomany.html
49 Canada's Jews, 358
50 None is Too Many, 278
51 Personal Policy Making, 85
52 None is Too Many, 278
53 Canada's Jews, 354
54 http://www.mfa.gov.il/MFA/MFAArchive/1990_1999/1999/5/FOCUS+on+Israel-+MACHAL+-+Overseas+Volunteers.htm
55 Personal Policy Making, 32

56 http://auto_sol.tao.ca/node/3047
57 Envoys Extraordinary, 44
58 Canada and the Birth of Israel, 237
59 Canada and the Birth of Israel, 140
60 Personal Policy Making, 30
61 Personal Policy Making, 30
62 Canada and the Birth of Israel, 225
63 Domestic Battleground, 31/137

Chapter 3

1 The Ethnic Cleansing of Palestine, 35
2 The Iron Cage, 1
3 1948, 181
4 The Making of the Arab-Israeli Conflict, 18
5 ZNet May 6 2008 (Dan Freeman-Maloy)
6 The Secret Army, 48
7 The Secret Army, 45
8 ZNet May 6 2008
9 The Secret Army, 37 & 45
10 The Secret Army, 44
11 Edgar Bronfman, 36
12 The Secret Army, 47
13 The Secret Army, 47-48
14 Domestic Battleground, 45
15 Dual Allegiance, 159
16 The Secret Army, 63
17 Canada's Jews, 364 & The Secret Army, 188
18 The Jews of Windsor, 136
19 The Secret Army, 62 & Fabled City, 155
20 By Way of Deception, 31
21 The Secret Army, 75
22 Bronfman Dynasty, 46
23 Hero, 143
24 http://www.thecanadianencyclopedia.com/index.cfm?PgNm=TCE&Params=A1A RTA0007550
25 1948, 370 & Righteous Victims, 247
26 Dual Allegiance, 159
27 Canada's Jews, 364
28 http://israelvets.com/pictorialhist_aiding_ground_forces.html
29 http://israelvets.com/pictorialhist_aiding_ground_forces.html
30 Dual Allegiance, 157
31 ZNet May 6 2008
32 The Secret Army, 64

33 The Secret Army, 118
34 ZNet May 6 2008
35 The Ethnic Cleansing of Palestine, 159
36 ZNet May 6 2008
37 The Birth of the Palestinian Refugee Problem Revisited, 481
38 ZNet May 6 2008
39 1949, 72
40 Dual Allegiance, 311
41 Dual Allegiance, 247 & 261
42 http://www.absoluteastronomy.com/topics/Ben_Dunkelman
43 Toronto Star Jun 12 1997
44 Globe & Mail Sep 25 1999
45 Image and Reality of the Israel Palestine Conflict, 86
46 Israeli Apartheid, 45
47 http://en.wikipedia.org/wiki/Present_absentee
48 http://en.wikipedia.org/wiki/Present_absentee
49 http://www.counterpunch.org/loewenstein01012009.html
50 Canada and the Birth of Israel, 209
51 Canada-Israel Friendship, 27
52 Canada and the Middle East, 12
53 Canadian Foreign Policy and the Palestine Problem, 13
54 The Fall and Rise of Israel, 383

Chapter 4

1 In the Strategic Interests of Canada, 39
2 In the Strategic Interests of Canada, 84
3 In the Strategic Interests of Canada, 82
4 In the Strategic Interests of Canada, 116
5 In the Strategic Interests of Canada, 117
6 In the Strategic Interests of Canada, 131
7 In the Strategic Interests of Canada, 133
8 http://www.questia.com/googleScholar.qst?docId=54014518
9 The Blue Berets, 11
10 The Commonwealth and Suez, 430
11 Nation Jul 6 2009
12 Canada-Israel Friendship, 36
13 United Nations Emergency Force, 73
14 The Commonwealth and Suez, 342
15 United Nations Emergency Force, 137
16 United Nations Emergency Force, 75

17 Canadian Foreign Policy and the Palestine Problem, 27
18 Canadian Foreign Policy and the Palestine Problem, 27
19 Canadian Foreign Policy and the Palestine Problem, 34
20 Canadian Foreign Policy and the Palestine Problem, 34
21 CIAA Vol VI # 5
22 Closely Guarded, 121
23 Canadian-Arab Relations, 65
24 Canada and the Third World, 254
25 Image and Reality of the Israel Palestine Conflict, 139
26 Image and Reality, 138
27 Image and Reality, 143
28 Canadian Foreign Policy and the Palestine Problem, 35
29 CIAA Vol VI #6
30 CIAA Vol VI #6
31 Canadian Foreign Policy and the Palestine problem, 39
32 Canadian Foreign Policy and the Palestine Problem, 40
33 Israel's Occupation, 6 & The End of the Peace Process, 270
34 Canadian Foreign Policy and the Palestine Problem, 43
35 Canadian Foreign Policy and the Palestine Problem, 41
36 Canadian Public Opinion and Government Policy Toward the Middle East, 3
37 Canadian Middle East Digest Vol 1 # 11
38 Canada and the Middle East, 45
39 Canadian Foreign Policy in the Middle East, 29
40 Le Canada et le conflit Israelo-Arab, 56
41 Social Praxis 1976/77 Vol 4/3 - 4, 282
42 Canada and the Middle East, 30
43 Canadian Middle East Digest Vol 1 # 16
44 From Lebanon to the Intifada, 23
45 From Lebanon to the Intifada, 23
46 From Lebanon to the Intifada, 24
47 Globe & Mail Dec 11 1982
48 Globe & Mail May 26 1983
49 Globe & Mail Sep 28 1981
50 Le Canada et le Conflit Israelo-Arab, 108

51 Defending the Holy Land, 183
52 Canadian-Arab Relations, 33
53 http://www.thetruthseeker.co.uk/print.asp?ID=187
54 Canadian-Arab Relations, 34
55 http://www.wrmea.com/backissues/0995/9509020.htm
56 From Lebanon to the Intifada, 35
57 From Lebanon to the Intifada, 35
58 Globe & Mail Sep 26 1981 & Oct 27 1988
59 Domestic Battleground, 198
60 Domestic Battleground, 191
61 Image and Reality, 140
62 Israel's Occupation, 193
63 Globe & Mail Dec 29 1981
64 Globe & Mail Jun 30 1983
65 Journal of Canadian Studies. 1992-93 Winter vol 27 #4, 11
66 Canadian Gunboat Diplomacy, 142; Canadian Foreign Policy, 387
67 Canada and the World Order, 207
68 http://news.bbc.co.uk/2/shared/spl/hi/middle_east/02/iraq_events/html/scuds.stm
69 Canada in NORAD, 148
70 http://www.wrmea.com/backissues/0391/9103041.htm
71 http://www.wrmea.com/backissues/0391/9103041.html

Chapter 5

1 Official Secrets, 279
2 Spy Wars, 197
3 Kill Khalid, 222/223
4 Official Secrets, 278
5 Washington report on Middle East Affairs Jan 1998, 26-27
6 http://www.wrmea.com/backissues/0794/9407057.htm
7 http://www.wrmea.com/backissues/0794/9407057.htm
8 http://www.wrmea.com/backissues/0794/9407057.htm
9 AP Nov 27 2002
10 http://www.zmag.org/znet/viewArticle/17552
11 Official Secrets, 13
12 Spy Wars, 250

13 Spy World, 154
14 Spy World, 154
15 http://www.wrmea.com/backissues/0198/9801026.htm
16 Canadian Jewish News Oct 22 1997
17 Kill Khalid, 221
18 Kill Khalid, 222
19 By Way of Deception, 74
20 http://www.lrb.co.uk/v31/n09/shtz01_.html
21 Canada and the Middle East, 12
22 Globe & Mail Nov 7 1997
23 Globe & Mail Nov 7 1997
24 Globe & Mail Nov 7 1997
25 Kill Khalid, 222
26 Kill Khalid, 222/223
27 Kill Khalid, 223
28 Washington Report on Middle East Affairs Jan 1998, 26-27
29 Kill Khalid, 225
30 Volunteers, 169
31 Kill Khalid, 228
32 Kill Khalid, 228
33 Globe & Mail Sep 6 1999
34 Globe & Mail Sep 6 1999
35 National Post Dec 24 2002
36 National Post Dec 24 2002
37 By Way of Deception, 162
38 By Way of Deception, 240
39 By Way of Deception, 240
40 Toronto Star Apr 8 2008
41 Canadian and Israeli Defense
42 http://www.cjpme.ca/documents/39%20En%20Canada Israel%20Public%20Safety%20Cooperation%20v.3.pdf
43 Canadian Jewish News Sep 8 2005
44 Canadian and Israeli Defense
45 Canadian Jewish News Sep 8 2005
46 Canadian Jewish News Jun 12 2008
47 Canadian Jewish News Jun 12 2008
48 Jerusalem Post Oct 22 2009
49 Jerusalem Post Oct 22 2009
50 This Magazine Sep 2005
51 Canadian and Israeli Defense
52 http://www.fromoccupiedpalestine.org/node/1589
53 Canadian and Israeli Defense
54 http://coat.ncf.ca/ARMX/cansec/all-3.htm
55 http://www.dominionpaper.ca/foreign_policy/2006/08/07/making_war.html
56 http://coat.ncf.ca/ARMX/cansec/Tables.htm
57 http://coat.ncf.ca/ARMX/cansec/Art_Dimension-May.htm
58 http://coat.ncf.ca/ARMX/cansec/Tables.htm
59 http://www.ciirdf.ca/press/news7_fr.html
60 http://coat.ncf.ca/ARMX/cansec/Tables.htm
61 http://www.socialistproject.ca/bullet/bullet176.html
62 Canadian and Israeli Defense
63 Canadian and Israeli Defense
64 Canadian and Israeli Defense
65 Canadian and Israeli Defense
66 La Presse Aug 8 2006
67 Canadian Jewish News Aug 24 2006
68 http://www.jewishtribune.ca/TribuneV2/index.php/200901061216/Prayer-services-held-for-local-men-seeing-Gaza-action.html
69 Canadian Jewish news Jul 30 2009
70 http://www.jewishtribune.ca/TribuneV2/index.php/20080527628/Chabad-Niagara-hosts-visting-IDF-heroes.html
71 www.jewishtribune.ca/TribuneV2/index.php/20080226410/IDF-search-and-rescue-officer-helps-open-new-Magen-David-Adom-chapter-raise-funds-for-ambulance.html
72 Canadian Jewish News Jun 18 2009
73 http://www.jewishtribune.ca/TribuneV2/index.php/200901281289/El-Al-offers-50-off-to-families-visiting-lone-Israeli-soldiers.html
74 http://www.caiaweb.org/files/indigo_leaflet_revised_june_07.pdf
75 History of B'nai B'rith Eastern Canada, 85
76 Domestic Battleground, 45
77 Domestic Battleground, 47
78 Domestic Battleground, 55
79 Canadian Jewish News Nov 16 2006
80 http://www.aecon.com/files/PDF/Investing_in_us/1999_AIF.pdf
81 Canadian Jewish News Oct 22 1998
82 http://www.merip.org/mer/mer216/216_halper.html

83 http://www.merip.org/mer/mer216/216_halper.html
84 http://www.nytimes.com/2004/10/04/opinion/04tarazi.html?_r=1
85 http://www.zmag.org/znet/viewArticle/826
86 Toronto Star Jul 11 2008
87 Toronto Star Jul 11 2008
88 Canadian and Israeli Defense
89 http://www.tadamon.ca/post/1235
90 http://www.tadamon.ca/post/2683 (Stefan Christoff)

Chapter 6

1 publicsafety.gc.ca
2 publicsafety.gc.ca
3 http://www.wrmea.com/archives/sept-oct02/0209043.html
4 Ottawa Citizen Nov 16 1991
5 Toronto Star Oct 13 1996
6 http://www.wrmea.com/archives/sept-oct02/0209043.html
7 Toronto Star Oct 13 1996
8 http://www.wrmea.com/backissues/0197/9701039.htm
9 National Post Nov 23 1999
10 Toronto Star Oct 13 1996
11 Toronto Star Oct 13 1996
12 Toronto Star Oct 13 1996
13 http://www.wrmea.com/backissues/0197/9701039.htm
14 http://www.wrmea.com/backissues/0197/9701039.htm
15 http://www.wrmea.com/backissues/0197/9701039.htm
16 National Post Sep 16 2002
17 Personal e-mail, David Drache
18 http://imeu.net/news/article001237.shtml
19 Canadian Jewish News Jun 16 1961
20 Domestic Battleground, 46
21 Saint John Telegraph Journal Mar 28 1998 & Jewish National Fund, 142
22 Canadian Dimension Feb 1981 & http://www.zmag.org/znet/viewArticle/21741
23 Toronto Star Jul 4 1995
24 http://chycho.gnn.tv/blogs/31104/In_1972_Canadians_donated_15_million_to_build_Canada_Park_on_destroyed_Palestinian_villages
25 http://www.counterpunch.org/cook06182009.html
26 http://www.wrmea.com/backissues/1091/9110034.htm
27 http://www.vcn.bc.ca/outlook/library/articles/israel/p05canada_park.htm & Vancouver Sun Jun 25 1992
28 http://www.nion.ca/jnf-forum-zayid.htm
29 http://www.nowtoronto.com/news/story.cfm?content=161040#
30 Now Magazine Dec 20 2007
31 http://one-state.net/quag11.html
32 http://www.wrmea.com/backissues/1091/9110034.htm
33 http://www.nowtoronto.com/news/story.cfm?content=161037
34 Canadian Jewish News Aug 30 2007
35 http://www.fromoccupiedpalestine.org/node/1419
36 Forward Feb 04 2005
37 Jewish National Fund, 147
38 Jewish National Fund, 148
39 Toronto Star Feb 13 1990
40 http://www.jewishtribune.ca/tribune/jt-051027-17.html
41 Canadian Jewish News Jul 2 2009
42 http://www.fromoccupiedpalestine.org/node/1419
43 Montreal Gazette May 23 2002
44 Canadian Jewish News Jul 2 2009
45 Globe & Mail Jun 27 1981
46 Globe & Mail Jun 27 1981
47 Globe & Mail Jun 27 1981
48 Globe & Mail Jun 27 1981
49 http://www.nion.ca/jnf-forum-zayid.htm
50 http://www.nion.ca/jnf-forum-zayid.htm
51 http://www.forward.com/articles/2854/
52 Canadian Jewish News Jan 4 2007
53 Canadian Jewish News May 25 2006
54 Canadian Jewish News May 26 2005
55 http://communications.uwo.ca/com/western_news/stories/western_president_honoured_by_jewish_organization_20071207440791/
56 Toronto Star Nov 19 2001
57 Canadian Jewish News Feb 10 1961
58 Canadian Jewish News Feb 26 2009

59 The Jews of Windsor, 148 & Canadian Jewish News Feb 12 1960
60 http://www.israelbonds.ca/who.asp
61 Financial Post Jul 27 1988
62 Financial Post Jul 27 1988
63 Montreal Gazette Aug 25 1993
64 Canadian Jewish News Feb 3 2000
65 Financial Post Jul 27 1988
66 Financial Post Jul 27 1988
67 Regards sur Israel Dec 1980
68 Montreal Gazette Jun 6 1990
69 Toronto Star Mar 19 1988
70 Canadian Jewish News May 26 1961
71 Canadian Jewish News May 26 1961
72 Domestic Battleground, 46
73 Canadian Jewish News Jun 16 1961
74 Canadian Jewish News May 27 1999
75 Canadian Jewish News Oct 12 2006
76 Canadian Jewish News Jul 2 2009
77 Canadian Jewish News Jul 2 2009
78 Canadian Jewish News Jul 4 1996
79 Regards sur Israel Apr 1998

Chapter 7

1 Le Canada et le conflit Israelo-Arab, 56
2 Canada and the Middle East, 30
3 Between the Wars, 142
4 Canadian Jewish News Feb 3 1961
5 Canadian Jewish News Mar 14 1969
6 Domestic Battleground, 199
7 Domestic Battleground, 208
8 http://www.washington-report.org/backissues/0693/9306057.htm
9 Domestic Battleground, 191
10 Canadian Foreign Policy, 36
11 Toronto Star Dec 17 1998
12 http://www.socialistproject.ca/bullet/bullet191.html
13 Canadian and Israeli Defense
14 Canadian Jewish News Jul 7 2005
15 Canadian and Israeli Defense
16 http://www.international.gc.ca/trade-agreements-accords-commerciaux/agr-acc/israel/part-1.aspx?lang=en
17 Canadian Jewish News Aug 21 1997
18 http://www.tadamon.ca/post/1235 & Canadian and Israeli Defense
19 Canadian and Israeli Defense
20 http://www.tadamon.ca/post/1235
21 Canadian Jewish News Jan 30 1997
22 Canadian Jewish News Mar 31 2005
23 Niagara Falls Review Mar 24 1999
24 Niagara Falls review Mar 24 1999
25 Globe & Mail Jul 19 1999
26 Globe & Mail Jul 19 1999
27 http://www.jewishvirtuallibrary.org/jsource/UN/weog1.html
28 http://www.washingtontimes.com/news/2001/jul/05/20010705-024132-4942r/
29 Canadian Jewish News Apr 6 2000
30 In/Security, 402
31 Canadian Jewish News Dec 7 2000
32 Human Rights and Democracy, 20
33 Canadian Jewish News Apr 25 2002
34 Ottawa Citizen Dec 18 2001
35 AP Nov 27 2002
36 http://www.zmag.org/znet/viewArticle/17552
37 Canadian Jewish News Nov 17 2005
38 http://www.shunpiking.com/ol0203/ZAYlet.htm
39 The Economist Oct 9 2003
40 Canadian Jewish News Jul 29 2004
41 Regina Leader Post Jul 10 2004
42 http://embassymag.ca/page/view/.2004.july.28.talking_points
43 Canadian Jewish News Jan 20 2005
44 Canadian Jewish News Dec 8 2005
45 http://www.embassymag.ca/page/view/jewish_vote-2-11-2009
46 Canada and the Birth of Israel, 19
47 Canada and Palestine, 80
48 Canadian Jewish News Feb 12 1998
49 Canada and the Birth of Israel, 37
50 Domestic Battleground, 44
51 Canada and Palestine, 69
52 Canada and Palestine, 70
53 This Magazine May 1988
54 This Magazine May 1988
55 Histadrut Campaign, National Archives
56 Canadian Jewish News Apr 22 1960
57 Canadian Jewish News Apr 22 1960
58 The Living Record of Canada's Partnership with Histadrut 1958, 2
59 http://www.arabmediawatch.com/amw/

CountryBackgrounds/Palestine/MediaMyths/
themyththatArabarmiestriedtowipeoutIsrael/
tabid/158/Default.aspx
60 Globe & Mail Nov 26 1979
61 http://electronicintifada.net/v2/
article10379.shtml
62 Righteous Victims, 119
63 Apartheid Israel, 113 & 118
64 http://electronicintifada.net/v2/
article10379.shtml
65 http://electronicintifada.net/v2/
article10379.shtml
66 Apartheid Israel, 110
67 Apartheid Israel, 113
68 Apartheid Israel, 114
69 This Magazine May 1988
70 Toronto Star May 16 1990
71 Toronto Star May 16 1990
72 Toronto Star May 16 1990
73 Canada-Israel Friendship, 137
74 Canada-Israel Friendship, 137
75 CIAA Jun 1967
76 Canada-Israel Friendship, 140
77 Canada-Israel Friendship, 141
78 Canadian Middle East Digest vol 1 #4
79 Canadian Middle East Digest vol 1 # 4
80 Domestic Battleground, 73
81 Canadian Middle East Digest vol 1 # 25
82 Canadian Middle East Digest vol 1 # 25
83 Canadian Labour Congress submission to
Parliamentary Special Joint Committee 1985
84 Globe and Mail Nov 26 1982
85 Canadian Middle East Digest Nov 1982
86 Canadian Middle East Digest Nov 1982
87 From Lebanon to the Intifada, 22
88 Globe & Mail Jun 27 1985
89 Toronto Star May 16 1990
90 Globe and Mail Sep 10 1985
91 Toronto Star May 16 1990
92 Canadian Jewish News Apr 28 2005
93 Canadian Jewish News Apr 28 2005
94 Canadian Jewish News Apr 28 2005
95 Canadian Jewish News Apr 28 2005
96 Hamilton Spectator Jun 7 2000
97 Hamilton Spectator Jun 7 2000
98 Canadian Jewish News Oct 2 2008
99 Canadian Jewish News Oct 21 2004
100 Canadian Jewish News Oct 21 2004
101 National Post Mar 6 2004
102 Canadian Jewish News Oct 2 2008
103 Winnipeg Sun Jan 9 2009

Chapter 8

1 Globe & Mail Jan 14 2008
2 Globe & Mail Aug 21 2009
3 http://www.israelnationalnews.com/News/
News.aspx/127730
4 Jewish Tribune July 22 2009
5 http://www.bnaibrith.org/latest_
news/2008-6-30_harper.cfm
6 Toronto Star Jun 1 2009
7 Montreal Gazette Jul 18 2006
8 Canada and the Middle East, 55
9 http://embassymag.ca/page/view/.2006.
august.23.lebanon
10 Toronto Star Feb 21 2008
11 Embassy Mag Feb 6 2008
12 New York Times Oct 26 2008
13 http://www.tadamon.ca/post/421
14 Montreal Gazette Nov 2 2006
15 http://electronicintifada.net/v2/
article6383.shtml
16 Canadian Jewish News Sep 10 2009
17 http://articles.latimes.com/2006/jul/13/
world/fg-hezbollah13
18 http://electronicintifada.net/v2/
article6383.shtml
19 http://www.pointdebasculecanada.ca/
breve/1513-quebec-une-depute-du-bloc-
agent-de-propagande-pour-le-hamas-et-
autres-djihadistes.php
20 Embassy Mag Nov 14 2007
21 http://embassymag.ca/page/
printpage/.2008.february.27.trade_deals
22 http://embassymag.ca/page/
printpage/.2008.february.27.trade_deals
23 http://embassymag.ca/page/view/.2005.
february.9.tp
24 National Post Oct 30 2009
25 Ottawa Citizen Nov 9 2007
26 Toronto Star Jan 23 2007
27 http://www.owensoundsuntimes.com/
ArticleDisplay.aspx?e=1457850
28 Wall Street Journal Feb 28 2009
29 Belleville EMC Sep 24 2009
30 Belleville EMC Sep 24 2009

31 Moncton Times Sep 23 2006
32 Globe & Mail Mar 11 2006
33 Canadian Jewish News Mar 16 2006
34 La Presse Jul 7 2006
35 Toronto Star Jan 20 2008 & National Post Jan 23 2008
36 The Economist Nov 29 2008
37 Globe & Mail Feb 25 2008
38 http://www.cjpac.ca/statements/read/24/397
39 http://www.cicweb.ca/scene/2009/03/canada-votes-against-anti-israel-resolutions-at-the-un-human-rights-council/
40 Canada and the Middle East, 91
41 Dominion Foreign Policy Issue, 27
42 http://www.embassymag.ca/page/view/bahdi-1-28-2009
43 Globe & Mail Oct 14 2006
44 Globe & Mail Oct 25 2006
45 http://www.ctv.ca/servlet/ArticleNews/story/CTVNews/20060214/harper_abbas_060214?s_name=tiff2006&no_ads=
46 Globe & Mail Mar 30 2007
47 http://embassymag.ca/issue/archive/2007/2007-04-04
48 http://embassymag.ca/issue/archive/2007/2007-04-04
49 Globe & Mail Jun 18 2007
50 Government of Canada press release Jul 23 2007
51 Government of Canada press release Jul 23 2007
52 http://www.cicweb.ca/relations/news_070723.cfm
53 Canadian Jewish News Nov 8 2007
54 Kill Khalid, 352
55 Kill Khalid, 352
56 Israel and the clash of civilizations, 129
57 Kill Khalid, 377
58 Canadian Dimension Jan 2008
59 Canadian Dimension Jan 2008
60 Moncton Times Jan 15 2008 & Globe & Mail Apr 11 2009
61 Wall Street Journal Oct 14 2009
62 Coalition to Oppose the Arms Trade Canada's secret war in Iraq
63 Globe & Mail Apr 11 2009
64 http://www.webofdemocracy.org/research/a_real_debate_about_r2p_fin.html
65 http://w01.international.gc.ca/MinPub/Publication.aspx?lang=eng&publication_id=386310&docnum=143
66 CBC News Dec 17 2007
67 Public Safety Canada Mar 24 2008
68 Moncton Times & Transcript Jan 15 2008 & http://www.jewishtribune.ca/TribuneV2/index.php/20080115319/Israel-Canada-friendship-strong-growing-Bernier-says.html
69 http://embassymag.ca/page/view/double_standard-3-11-2009
70 Saint John Telegraph-Journal Jan 15 2008
71 Moncton Times Jan 15 2008
72 Canadian Jewish News Jan 31 2008
73 http://embassymag.ca/page/view/cida_gaza-7-22-2009
74 http://embassymag.ca/page/view/cida_gaza-7-22-2009
75 http://www.jewishtribune.ca/TribuneV2/index.php/200906161765/Canada-aims-to-help-stem-flow-of-illicit-weapons-into-Gaza.html
76 Canadian Jewish News Jun 18 2009
77 Toronto Star Mar 17 2008
78 Toronto Star Mar 17 2008
79 National Post Jan 7 2009
80 Toronto Star Jan 7 2009
81 Globe & Mail Jan 7 2009
82 Globe & Mail Jan 7 2009
83 http://www.dissidentvoice.org/2009/03/made-in-israel-foreign-policy-puts-canadian-lives-at-risk/
84 http://www.dissidentvoice.org/2009/03/made-in-israel-foreign-policy-puts-canadian-lives-at-risk/
85 http://embassymag.ca/page/view/canada_israel_venezuela_visas-8-5-2009 & http://www.dominionpaper.ca/articles/2526
86 Jewish Tribune Aug 5 2009
87 http://www.iran-daily.com/1387/3323/pdf/i3.pdf
88 Le Devoir Jan 23 2009
89 http://embassymag.ca/page/printpage/.2008.july.2.israel
90 http://embassymag.ca/page/printpage/.2008.july.2.israel

Chapter 9

1 http://www.bloomberg.com/apps/news?pid=20601082&sid=axPErVMKTpsg

2 Walrus Magazine Oct 2006

3 Allies for Armageddon, 282

4 Walrus Oct 2006

5 Canadian Jewish News May 22 2008

6 Canada NewsWire May 7 2008

7 http://www.bnaibrith.ca/article.php?id=399

8 http://www.cufi.org/site/PageServer?pagename=events_nights_to_honor_israel_reports#toronto_may_3_2008

9 Walrus Oct 2006

10 Walrus Oct 2006

11 Canadian Jewish News Jun 12 2008

12 Canadian Jewish News Jun 12 2008

13 Canadian Jewish News Jun 12 2008

14 Canadian Jewish News Feb 15 2001

15 Canadian Jewish News Feb 15 2001

16 Canadian Jewish News Feb 15 2001

17 Canadian Jewish News Jun 5 2008

18 Canadian Jewish News Mar 13 2003

19 Canadian Jewish News Mar 13 2003

20 Canadian Jewish News Mar 13 2003

21 Canadian Jewish News Mar 13 2003

22 http://www.israelmybeloved.com/channel/israel_today/section/commerce_industry

23 Canadian Jewish News May 22 2008

24 http://www.canada.com/topics/travel/story.html?id=5080377f-0938-4c7e-9a49-b66d2693f037

25 http://www.jewishtribune.ca/TribuneV2/index.php/20080430565/-Visit-Israel.-Youll-never-be-the-same-Christians-urged.html

26 http://www.jewishtribune.ca/TribuneV2/index.php/20080430565/-Visit-Israel.-Youll-never-be-the-same-Christians-urged.html & Evangelicals and Israel, 218

27 Canadian Jewish News Feb 15 2007

28 Canadian Jewish News Feb 15 2007

29 Christian attitudes towards the State of Israel, 200

30 Canadian Jewish News Apr 19 2001

31 Canadian Jewish News Apr 19 2001

32 http://www.jewishtribune.ca/tribune/jt-051027-03.html

33 Canadian Jewish News Apr 19 2001

34 Canadian Jewish News Apr 19 2001

35 Canadian Jewish News Apr 14 2005

36 Canadian Jewish News Mar 13 2003

37 Walrus Oct 2006

38 Walrus Oct 2006

39 http://dennisgruending.ca/pulpitandpolitics/2009/10/05/canadian-evangelical-voting-trends/

40 Brantford Expositor Oct 18 2004

41 Canadian Jewish News Jan 24 2008

42 Canadian Jewish News Jan 24 2008

43 Walrus Oct 2006

44 http://www.jpost.com/servlet/Satellite?cid=1170359780973&pagename=JPost%2FJPArticle%2FShowFull

45 http://www.jpost.com/servlet/Satellite?cid=1170359780973&pagename=JPost%2FJPArticle%2FShowFull

46 Christian Zionism, 162

47 Allies for Armageddon, 274

48 Hamilton Spectator Aug 29 2005

49 Hamilton Spectator Aug 29 2005

50 Walrus Oct 2006

51 http://www.jewishtribune.ca/TribuneV2/index.php/20080521619/-Israel-cannot-pull-out-anymore-pastor-declares.html

52 Christian Zionism, 101

53 http://www.jewishtribune.ca/TribuneV2/index.php/20080124344/Christian-Zionists-more-consistent-supporters-of-Israel-than-Jews-evangelist-believes.html

54 Christian Attitudes Towards the State of Israel, 204

55 Montreal Gazette Jun 4 2000

56 Toronto Star Nov 3 2009

57 Ottawa Citizen Apr 21 2009

58 http://www.haaretz.com/hasen/spages/1087973.html

59 Canwest News May 8 2008

60 Canadian Jewish News Oct 1 2009

61 Canadian Jewish News Jun 11 2009 & Jewish Tribune Jul 2 2009

62 Canadian Jewish News Jul 5 2007

63 http://www.jewishtribune.ca/TribuneV2/index.php/200907021811/Canada-achieves-full-membership-in-International-Holocaust-Task-Force.html

64 Canadian Jewish news Feb 26 2009
65 http://www.cpcca.ca/about.htm
66 Canadian Jewish news Jun 11 2009
67 Jewish Tribune Sep 30 2009
68 Canadian Jewish News Jun 14 2007
69 Canadian Jewish News Jun 14 2007
70 Canadian Jewish News Jun 14 2007
71 Canadian Jewish News Mar 7 2002
72 Canadian Jewish News Mar 7 2002
73 Canadian Jewish News Jun 14 2007
74 Canadian Jewish News Jun 14 2007
75 Canadian Jewish News Jun 14 2007
76 http://www.jewishtribune.ca/tribune/jt-051006-02.html
77 Silent Partners, 271
78 Canadian Jewish News Jul 3 1997
79 http://www.jewishtribune.ca/TribuneV2/index.php/20080506573/The-delayed-reaction-to-the-Holocaust.html
80 http://www.jewishtribune.ca/TribuneV2/index.php/20080506573/The-delayed-reaction-to-the-Holocaust.html
81 Delayed Impact, 151
82 Delayed Impact, 161
83 Delayed Impact, 175
84 Asper Nation, 173
85 National Post Nov 17 2008
86 Asper Nation, 175
87 Asper Nation, 175
88 Asper Nation, 200
89 Asper Nation, 131
90 Asper Nation, 132
91 Asper Nation, 131
92 Asper Nation, 215
93 http://www.nytimes.com/2004/09/20/business/media/20reuters.html?_r=1
94 Toronto Star Jul 3 1995
95 Domestic Battleground, 239
96 http://www.embassymag.ca/page/view/jewish_vote-2-11-2009
97 http://www.jewishtribune.ca/tribune/jt-051110-03.html
98 Montreal Gazette Sep 23 1986
99 http://www.afn.ca/article.asp?id=2276
100 http://www.canada.com/victoriatimescolonist/story.html?id=a280f582-06dc-42f8-b5fc-5af369f7a6ef
101 http://www.jewishtribune.ca/tribune/jt-060112-11.html
102 Canadian Jewish News Aug 7 2008
103 Canadian Jewish News Jul 31 2008
104 http://www.rabble.ca/news/exposed-university-toronto-suppressed-pro-palestinian-activism
105 http://www.rabble.ca/news/exposed-university-toronto-suppressed-pro-palestinian-activism
106 http://www.rabble.ca/news/exposed-university-toronto-suppressed-pro-palestinian-activism
107 http://www.socialistproject.ca/bullet/bullet191.html
108 http://www.socialistproject.ca/bullet/bullet191.html
109 http://www.jewishtribune.ca/TribuneV2/index.php/20080115321/Power-couple-take-Manitoban-and-Israeli-student-learning-to-a-new-level.html
110 http://www.jewishtribune.ca/TribuneV2/index.php/20080115321/Power-couple-take-Manitoban-and-Israeli-student-learning-to-a-new-level.html
111 Montreal Gazette Sep 26 2002
112 Concordia Link Jan 7 2003
113 Asper Nation, 176
114 Canadian Jewish News Sep 2 1999
115 NewsWire Nov 22 2000
116 http://magazine.carleton.ca/2000_spring/162.htm
117 Fabled City, 161
118 http://www.globecampus.ca/in-the-news/article/schulich-donates-20-million-to-dalhousie-law-school/
119 Canadian Jewish News Dec 11 1997
120 Canadian Jewish News Dec 11 1997
121 Canadian Jewish News Jun 26 2003
122 http://www.torontolife.com/features/yorks-middle-east-war/?pageno=3
123 http://www.torontolife.com/features/yorks-middle-east-war/?pageno=3
124 Fateful Triangle, 21
125 Fateful Triangle, 21
126 Montreal Gazette Apr 3 2008
127 Montreal Gazette Apr 3 2008
128 Toronto Star Dec 8 1985

129 National Post Oct 14 2006
130 Journal of Canadian Studies 1992-93
Winter vol. 27 # 4, 14
131 Canada and the Arab-Israeli Conflict, 55
132 Canada and the Arab-Israeli Conflict, 55
133 http://www.jewishvirtuallibrary.org/
jsource/myths/canada.html
134 Domestic Battleground, 196
135 Lightning Rods Rather Than Light
Switches
136 Le Canada et le Conflit Israelo-Arab, 79
137 Lightning Rods Rather Than Light
Switches
138 Domestic Battleground, 31 & 137
139 In the Strategic Interests of Canada, 52
140 In the Strategic Interests of Canada, 52
141 Canada Israel Reporter Feb/Mar 1956
142 http://unispal.un.org/UNISPAL.NSF/0/
E4F17C62FF03C9CE8525749400667701
143 Canada Middle East Digest Nov 1986
144 http://www.haaretz.com/hasen/
spages/1087973.html

Chapter 10

1 Montreal Gazette Jan 11 2009
2 Globe & Mail Feb 10 2009
3 Globe & Mail Feb 1 2005
4 http://www.counterpunch.org/
walberg10192009.html & Canadian Jewish
News Aug 27 2009
5 Canadian Jewish News Aug 27 2009
6 Canadian Jewish News Aug 27 2009
7 http://auto_sol.tao.ca/node/2304
8 http://electronicintifada.net/bytopic/486.
shtml
9 Ambiguous Champion, 48
10 http://www.labournet.net/ukunion/0909/
tucpal5.html
11 Reuters Sep 3 2009
12 http://adalahny.org/index.php/
press-releases/25-press-releases-land-
developer/319-report-and-statement-
indicate-that-tiaa-cref-has-divested-from-
africa-israel

Bibliography

A Coat of Many Colors: two centuries of Jewish life in Canada. Irving Abella, Key Porter books (1990)

Allies for Armageddon: the rise of Christian Zionism. Victoria Clark, Yale University Press (2007)

All That Remains: the Palestinian villages occupied and depopulated by Israel in 1948. Walid Khalidi, Institute for Palestine Studies (1992)

An Olive Branch on the Family Tree: the Arabs in Canada. Baha Abu-Laban, McClelland & Stewart (1980)

Apartheid Israel: Possibilities for the Struggle Within. Uri Davis, Zed (2003)

Asper Nation: Canada's Most Dangerous Media Company. Marc Edge, New Star Books (2007)

The Ambiguous Champion: Canada and South Africa in the Trudeau and Mulroney years. Linda Freeman, University Of Toronto Press (1997)

Between Arab and Israeli. ELM Burns, Ivan Obolensky Inc. (1962)

Between the Wars: Canadian Jews in transition. Israel Medres, Vehicle Press (1964)

The Birth of the Palestinian Refugee Problem Revisited. Benny Morris, Cambridge University Press (2004)

The Blue Berets: the Story of the United Nations Peacekeeping Forces. Michael Harbottle, Leo Cooper (1975)

Branching Out: The Transformation of the Canadian Jewish Community. Gerald Tulchinsky, Stoddart (1998)

Bronfman Dynasty. Peter C. Newman, McClelland & Stewart (1978)

By Way of Deception. Victor Ostrovsky and Claire Hoy, St. Martin's Press (1990)

Canada and Palestine: The Politics of Non-Commitment. Zachariah Kay, Israel University Press (1978)

Canada and the Arab-Israeli conflict [microform]: a study of the Yom Kippur War and the domestic political environment. David Taras, LAC Catalogue, Canadian Libraries (1985)

Canada and the Birth of Israel: A Study in Canadian Foreign Policy. David J Bercuson, University of Toronto Press (1985)

Canada and the Middle East: In Theory and Practice. Paul Heinebecker and Momani Bessma, Wilfrid Laurier University Press (2007)

Canada and the Middle East: The Foreign Policy of a Client State. Tareq Y Ismael, Detselig Enterprises (1994)

Canada and the New World Order. Michael J. Tucker, Irwin Publishing (2000)

Canada-Israel Friendship. Shira Herzog Bessin and David Kaufman, Canada-Israel Committee (1979)

Canada in NORAD: 1957-2007: a history. Joseph T Jockel McGill-Queen's University Press (2007)

Canada Middle East Relations: The end of Liberal-Internationalism. David B Dewitt and John Kirton in Janice Stein and David Dewitt, eds., The Middle East in Crisis: Internal Forces and External Powers, Mosaic Press (1983)

Canada's Jews: a People's journey. Gerald Tulchinsky, University of Toronto Press (2008)

Canadian-Arab Relations: Policy and Perspectives. Tareq Y Ismael, Jerusalem International publishing house (1984)

Canadian and Israeli Defense — Industrial and Homeland Security Ties: An Analysis. Kole Kilibarda (2009)

Canadian Foreign Policy and the Palestine Problem. Ali Dessouki, Middle East Research Center Publication (1969)

Canadian Foreign Policy in the Middle East: a summary. Canada Israel Committee (1976)

Canadian Foreign Policy: selected cases. Don Munton and John Kirton, Orentice Hall Canada (1992)

Canadian Gunboat Diplomacy: The Canadian Navy and Foreign Policy. Ann L Griffi ths & Peter T Haydon & Richard H Gimblett, Center for Foreign Policy Studies, Dalhousie University (2000)

Canadian Maverick: the life and times of Ivan C. Rand. William Kaplan, University of Toronto Press (2009)

Canadian Public Opinion and Government Policy Toward the Middle East. Jack Zubrzycki, Near Eastern Cultural and Educational Foundation of Canada (1986)

Christian Zionism: Road-map to Armageddon? Stephen R. Sizer, Inter Varsity Press (2004)

Christian Attitudes Towards the State of Israel. Paul C Merkley, McGill Queen's University Press (2001)

The Commonwealth and Suez: a documentary survey. James George Eayrs, Oxford University Press (1964)

Closely Guarded: a life in Canadian security and intelligence. John Starnes, University of Toronto Press (1998)

Defending the Holy Land: A Critical Analysis Of Israel's Security & Foreign Policy. Zeev Maoz, University of Michigan Press (2006)

Delayed Impact: the Holocaust and the Canadian Jewish Community. Franklin Bialystok, McGill-Queen's University Press (2000)

Dialogue for Development: Israel's Foreign Assistance Programme. David M. Weinberg, Canada-Israel Committee (1986)

The Domestic Battleground: Canada and the Israeli Conflict. David Taras and David H Goldberg, McGill-Queens University Press (1989)

Domestic Determinants of Foreign Policy: Newly Immigrated Ethnic Communities and the Canadian Foreign Policy-Making Process, 1984-1993. Roy Brent Norton, UMI Dissertation Services (1999)

Dual Allegiance: An Autobiography. Ben Dunkelman, Macmillan of Canada (1976)

Edgar Bronfman: the making of a Jew. Edgar Bronfman, Putnam Adult (1996)

The End of the Peace Process: Oslo and after. Edward W. Said, Vintage Books (2001)

Envoys Extraordinary: women of the Canadian foreign service. Margaret Weiers, Dundurn Press (1995)

The Ethnic Cleansing of Palestine. Ilan Pappé, One World Publications (2006)

Evangelicals and Israel: the story of American Christian Zionism. Stephen Spector, Oxford University Press (2009)

Fabled City: The Jews Of Montreal. Joe King, Price-Patterson (2009)

The Fall and Rise of Israel: the story of the Jewish people during the time of their dispersal and regathering. William L Hull, Zondervan (1954)

Fateful Triangle: the United States, Israel, and the Palestinians. Noam Chomsky, Black Rose Books (1999)

The Foreign Policy of the New Democratic Party, 1961-1988. Lloyd Norman Penner, National Library of Canada (1996)

For the Time is at Hand: an account of the prophecies of Henry Wentworth Monk of Ottawa, friend of the Jews. Richard S. Lambert, London (1947)

From Immigration to Integration: the Canadian Jewish experience. Ruth Klein and Frank Dimant, Institute for International Affairs B'nai B'rith Canada (2001)

From Lebanon to the Intifada: the Jewish Lobby and Canadian Middle East Policy. Ronnie Miller, University Press of America (1991)

From Mandate to State, 1923-1948: history of Zionist order habonim. Bernard Figler, Montreal (1951)

Hero: the Buzz Beurling story. Brian Nolan, Lester and Orpen Dennys (1981)

History of B'nai B'rith Eastern Canada. B'nai B'rith, (1964)

History of Zionist ideal in Canada. Bernard Figler, Montreal (1962)

Human Rights and Democracy: Issues for Canadian Policy in Democracy Promotion. Nancy Thede, IRPP (2005)

Image and Reality of the Israel Palestine Conflict. Norman G. Finkelstein Verso (2001)

In/Security: Canada in the Post 9/11 World. Allen Seager & Alexander N Etherton & Karl Froschauer, Center for Canadian Studies, Simon Fraser University (2005)

In the Strategic Interests of Canada: Canadian Arms Sales to Israel and Other Middle East States, 1949-1956. Barry Bristman, MA thesis, University of Calgary (1992)

The Iron Cage: the story of the Palestinian struggle for statehood. Rashid Khalidi, Beacon Press (2006)

Israel and the Clash of Civilizations. Jonathan Cook, Pluto (2008)

Israel and the Western powers: 1952-1960. Zach Levey, University of North Carolina Press (1997)

Israeli Apartheid: a beginner's guide. Ben White, Pluto (2009)

Israel's Occupation. Neve Gordon, University of California Press (2008)

Inside Canadian Intelligence: exposing the new realities of espionage and international terrorism. Dwight Hamilton, Dundurn Press (2006)

Jewish National Fund. Walter Lehn & Uri Davis, Chapman & Hall (1988)

The Jews of Windsor, 1790-1990: a historical chronicle. Jonathan Plautm, Dundurn Press (2008)

Kill Khalid: the failed Mossad assassination of Khalid Mishal and the rise of Hamas. Paul McGeough, W.W. Norton & Co. (2009)

The Lebanese Crisis: 1958. M.S Agwani, Asia Publishing House (1965)

Le Canada et le Conflit Israelo-Arab depuis 1947. Houchang Hassan-Wari, Harmattan (1997)

Le Mouvement ouvrier Juif au Canada, 1904-1920. Pierre Anctil, Septentrion (1999)

Lightning Rods Rather Than Light Switches: Arab Economic Sanctions against Canada in 1979. Norrin M. Ripsman & Jean-Marc F. Blanchard, Canadian Journal of Political Science, Vol 35, Issue 01, (March 2002)

Lillian and Archie Freiman: biographies. Bernard Figler (1959)

Louis Fitch Q. C.. Bernard Figler (1968)

The Living Record of Canada's Partnership with Histadrut 1958. Canadian Association for Labor Israel (1958)

The Making of the Arab-Israeli Conflict, 1947-51. Ilan Pappé, I.B. Tauris and Co. (1992)

None is Too Many: Canada and the Jews of Europe, 1933-1948. Irving Abella and Harold Troper, Keiy Porter Books (2000)

Non-Jewish Zionism: its roots in Western history. Regina S. Sherif, Zed (1983)

Official Secrets: the story behind the Canadian Security Intelligence Service. Richard Cleroux, McGraw-Hill (1990)

One Palestine, Complete: Jews and Arabs Under the British Mandate. Tom Segev, Owl Books (2001)

The Origins of Canadian Foreign Policy Towards the Arab-Israeli conflict: a question of influence?. Christine Allan, National Library of Canada (1997)

Palestine: peace not apartheid. Jimmy Carter, Simon & Schuster (2006)

Pearson's Prize: Canada and the Suez Crisis. John Melady, Dundurn Press (2006)

Personal Policy Making: Canada's role in the adoption of the Palestine Partition Resolution. Eliezer Tauber, Greenwood Press (2002)

Rabbi Dr. Herman Abramowitz, Lazarus Cohen, Lyon Cohen. Bernard Figler, Harpell Press (1968)

Righteous Victims: A history of the Zionist-Arab conflict, 1881-1999. Benny Morris, Knopf (1999)

The Rise and Fall of a Middle Power: Canadian diplomacy from King to Mulroney. Arthur Andrew, Lorimer (1993)

The Secret Army. David J Bercuson, Lester and Orpen Dennys (1993)

Seize the Day: Lester B Pearson and Crisis Diplomacy. Geoffrey AH Pearson, Carleton University Press (1993)

Silent Partners: taxpayers and the bankrolling of Bombardier. Peter Hadekel, Key Porter Books (2004)

Spy Wars: Espionage and Canada from Gouzenko to Glasnost. J. L. Granatstein and David Stafford, Key Porter Books (1990)

Spy World: inside the Canadian and American intelligence establishments. Mike Frost and Michel Gratton, Doubleday Canada Ltd. (1994)

Taking Root: the origins of the Canadian Jewish community. Gerald Tulchinsky, Stoddart (1992)

United Nations Emergency Force. Gabriella Rosner, Columbia University Press (1963)

The Volunteer: A Canadian's Secret Life in the Mossad. Michael Ross & Jonathan Kay, McClelland & Stewart (2007)

Western Imperialism in the Middle East: 1914-1958. David Kenneth Fieldhouse, Oxford University Press (2006)

1948: a history of the first Arab-Israeli war. Benny Morris, Yale University Press (2008)

1949, The First Israelis. Tom Segev, Owl Books (1998)

Resources for Activists
Organizations

Solidarity for Palestinian Human Rights (13 campus chapters)
http://www.sphr.org/v3/ email: info@sphr.org
(514) 999-1948

Coalition Against Israeli Apartheid (6 cities)
www.caiaweb.org email: endapartheid@riseup.net (647)
831-5516

Independent Jewish Voices - Canada (7 cities)
www.independentjewishvoices.ca/ email: shniad@gmail.com

Students Against Israeli Apartheid (3 campus chapters)
http://saia.ca/

Tadamon! (Montreal)
www.tadamon.ca email: info@tadamon.ca 514-664-1036

Canadians for Justice and Peace in the Middle East
http://www.cjpme.org/ email: info@cjpme.org
(514) 745-8491

Canada Palestine Support Network
www.canpalnet.ca

Not in Our Name — Jewish Voices Against Israel's Wars
http://www.nion.ca/
email: info@nion.ca or nion.ottawa@gmail.com

Canada Palestine Association (Vancouver)
www.cpavancouver.org/

Sumoud Political Prisoner Solidarity Group
http://sumoud.tao.ca/

Jews for a Just Peace (Vancouver)
www.jewsforajustpeace.com/

Students for Palestinian Rights (Waterloo)
http://sfpr.uwaterloo.ca/

Resources for Activists
Websites and magazines

Canadian:
www.dominionpaper.ca
www.rabble.ca
Canadian Dimension magazine
Briarpatch magazine
New Socialist magazine
Press for Conversion
Outlook magazine
General:
Electronicintifada.net
www.zmag.org
counterpunch.org

About the Author

Former Vice President of the Concordia Student Union, Yves Engler is a Montreal activist and author. He has three previously published books: *The Black Book of Canadian Foreign Policy* (Shortlisted for the Mavis Gallant Prize for Non Fiction in the Quebec Writers' Federation Literary Awards), *Playing Left Wing: From Rink Rat to Student Radical* and (with Anthony Fenton) *Canada in Haiti: Waging War on The Poor Majority*.